# Joseph Smith's
First Vision

# Joseph Smith's First Vision

## A Guide to the Historical Accounts

### Steven C. Harper

DESERET BOOK

Salt Lake City, Utah

© 2012 Steven Craig Harper

All rights reserved. No part of this book may be reproduced in any form or by any means without permission in writing from the publisher, Deseret Book Company, P. O. Box 30178, Salt Lake City, Utah 84130. This work is not an official publication of The Church of Jesus Christ of Latter-day Saints. The views expressed herein are the responsibility of the author and do not necessarily represent the position of the Church or of Deseret Book Company.

DESERET BOOK is a registered trademark of Deseret Book Company.

Visit us at DeseretBook.com

**Library of Congress Cataloging-in-Publication Data**

Harper, Steven Craig, 1970– author.
  Joseph Smith's First Vision : a guide to the historical accounts / Steven C. Harper.
      pages cm
  Includes bibliographical references and index.
  ISBN 978-1-60907-154-7 (hardbound : alk. paper)
  1. Smith, Joseph, 1805–1844—First Vision.  2. The Church of Jesus Christ of Latter-day Saints—History—19th century.  3. The Church of Jesus Christ of Latter-day Saints—Doctrines. 4. Mormon Church—History—19th century.  5. Mormon Church—Doctrines.  6. New York (State)—Church history—19th century.  I. Title.
  BX8695.S6H28 2012
  289.3092—dc23                                                                    2012033595

Printed in the United States of America
Publishers Printing, Salt Lake City, UT

10  9  8  7  6  5  4  3  2  1

*For*

*Elder Marlin K. Jensen,*

*Church Historian, disciple of Christ,*

*"and for the rising generations"*

*(D&C 69:8)*

# Contents

———⇒•⇐———

List of Color Plates . . . . . . . . . . . . . . . . . . . . ix

Introduction . . . . . . . . . . . . . . . . . . . . . . . . 1

1. Seeking, Assuming, and Knowing . . . . . . . . . . . . 3

2. Joseph Smith's Family and Culture . . . . . . . . . . . 13

3. "The Lord Opened the Heavens upon Me" . . . . . . 23

4. A Well-Documented Theophany . . . . . . . . . . . . 31

5. Three Critiques of Joseph Smith's Testimony . . . . . 67

6. Listening to Joseph Smith Communicate . . . . . . . 84

7. Listening to Joseph Smith Remember . . . . . . . . . 94

8. Seekers Wanted . . . . . . . . . . . . . . . . . . . . . 111

Index . . . . . . . . . . . . . . . . . . . . . . . . . . . . 125

# Color Plates

―――→•←―――

Plate 1   Joseph Smith, Letterbook 1, cover

Plate 2   Joseph Smith, Letterbook 1, page 1

Plate 3   Joseph Smith, Letterbook 1, page 2

Plate 4   Joseph Smith, Letterbook 1, page 3

Plate 5   Joseph Smith, Letterbook 1, page 3, detail

Plate 6   Frederick G. Williams

Plate 7   Joseph Smith, 1835–1836 Journal, cover

Plate 8   Joseph Smith, 1835–1836 Journal, page 23

Plate 9   Joseph Smith, 1835–1836 Journal, page 24

Plate 10   Joseph Smith, History, volume A-1, cover

Plate 11   Joseph Smith, History, volume A-1, page 1

COLOR PLATES

Plate 12   Joseph Smith, History, volume A-1, page 2

Plate 13   Joseph Smith, History, volume A-1, page 3

Plate 14   Joseph Smith, History, volume A-1, page 3

Plate 15   Joseph Smith, History, volume A-1, pages 132–33

Plate 16   Joseph Smith, History, volume A-1, page 4

Plate 17   Levi Richards, Journal, entry for 11 June 1843

Plate 18   Alexander Neibaur, Journal, entry for 24 May 1844

# Introduction

I once listened to a presentation by several highly regarded historians. They had been asked if they could witness any single event in American history, which they would choose and why. Some of the answers were profound. One scholar thought of Columbus on the morning of discovery. Another said the closed debates of the Constitutional Convention. Other answers struck me as silly or insignificant.

No one asked me, but I knew from the moment I heard the question what my answer would be. I would be present for Joseph Smith's vision in the woods of western New York. A later Church president, Joseph F. Smith, regarded it as the most significant historical event since the Savior's resurrection.[1]

No wonder it is hotly contested. On the one hand, Joseph Smith's first vision may be the best-documented theophany—vision of God—in history. Joseph Smith's papers include four or five different accounts (depending on how one decides to identify them). Most of these were later copied at least once.

---

1. Joseph F. Smith, *Gospel Doctrine,* 5th ed. (Salt Lake City: Deseret Book, 1939), 495–96.

There are also a few contemporary secondary accounts in the papers of people who heard him tell of it. On the other hand, critics contend that the multiple accounts are inconsistent with each other or with historical facts and see in them an evolving story that Joseph embellished over time. The very same evidence sustains a more faithful view. The multiple accounts and the historical facts do not compel one to disbelieve Joseph. Some, in fact, find the richly documented vision a compelling reason to believe him.

It is the potential power of Joseph's claims that makes them controversial. Historians get worked up in debates about the origins of revolutions or civil wars, but none of that compares to what is at stake with Joseph's vision. In this case the maxim rings true: Joseph's vision is not a matter of life or death; it's much more important than that. This book, therefore, takes the vision seriously. It considers all the known evidence that originated with Joseph Smith, the only witness to the event, and it does so in a particular way. It is not a doubting book but neither is it a defensive or a dogmatic one. It seeks truth by study and by faith (D&C 88:118), and it is written for a particular group of readers, namely "inquirers, seekers after truth."[2]

---

2. J. Reuben Clark Jr., "The Charted Course of the Church in Education," address to LDS seminary and institute leaders, 8 August 1938, http://president.byu.edu/documents/clark.htm, accessed 17 June 2012. See Henry B. Eyring, *To Draw Closer to God* (Salt Lake City: Deseret Book, 1997), 144.

CHAPTER 1

# Seeking, Assuming, and Knowing

In philosophical terms, Joseph Smith's first vision is epistemological. Epistemology is the philosophy of knowing. It seeks answers to such questions as: What is knowledge? What do I know? How do I know? Joseph's vision is about knowing. "How to act I did not know," he said about his pre-vision self. But after the vision he knew. "I had seen a vision, I knew it, and I knew that God knew it" (1838 account; see chapter 4).

This book is also epistemological. It asks, What can be known of Joseph's experience and how? It seeks answers based on the historical method and on spiritual experience. We who seek to know the veracity of Joseph's testimony can know only through Joseph. He was the only witness. He created the evidence we have to evaluate. When studying the vision, it is best to *seek* learning by faithfully studying Joseph's accounts. It is worst to *assume* what his experience must have been like and how he would respond to it. But that's exactly what many people do, including many who believe in Joseph's vision. They create hypothetical history that is easily disproved. For example, without ever analyzing the evidence closely, some assume that if a teenage boy saw God and Christ, he would obviously tell his family right away. Certainly he would remember the date of the event and his precise age at the time. Undoubtedly he would write down the experience immediately. And surely he would relate it the same way every time he told it. Yet not one of those assumptions is supported by the historical record—the accounts that come to us from Joseph.

Joseph Smith's epistemology—the seeking way of knowing he described and enacted in the grove—can be our way of knowing. In other words, if we seek as Joseph did, we can come to know what he knew as he knew it. Probably the best known statement of this seeking way of knowing is Moroni 10:3–5 in the Book of Mormon. We sometimes hear this passage summed up as "just pray about it," but those four words are hardly an adequate summary of the scripture's more than one hundred carefully chosen words. Rather, Moroni enjoins his readers to act in specific ways and to act upon the testimonies captured in and communicated by the Book of Mormon. These two ingredients—the testimony itself and our ability to independently test its veracity—are essential to this epistemological recipe. We must have the testimony in order to verify it. But simply knowing about a testimony is not the same as knowing whether it is true. Thus, Moroni invites those who read the testimony to remember and to ponder it. This is a call for brainwork: reading, remembering, pondering—all with real intent, or focused purpose. To this, Moroni continues, add spiritual longings and capacities: faith, sincerity, prayer to God in the name of Jesus Christ. When the seeker invests all of the required elements—intellectual and spiritual—the promise is that "by the power of the Holy Ghost ye may know the truth of all things" (Moroni 10:5).

An early Latter-day Saint newspaper article explained this way of knowing: "Search the revelations which we publish, and ask your heavenly Father, in the name of his Son Jesus Christ, to manifest the truth unto you, and if you do it with an eye single to his glory, nothing doubting, he will answer you by the power of his Holy Spirit: You will then know for yourselves and not for another: You will not then be dependent on man for the knowledge of God."[1] Elder Dallin H. Oaks described this way of knowing as the "principle of independent verification by revelation." This is seeking. It is Mormon epistemology. "We encourage everyone to study the scriptures," Elder Oaks declared, "and to prayerfully seek personal revelation to know their meanings for themselves."[2]

Certainly there are alternative ways of thinking about knowledge. Enlightenment rationalism and the scientific method emphasize observation and the intellect but discount spiritual possibilities or other dimensions of knowing. These epistemologies are good at knowing proximate truths but fail when it comes to knowing ultimate meanings, or verifying the existence of God or whether he appeared to Joseph in a grove. These rational, scientific ways of knowing are appealing. They provide satisfying certainty about many historically perplexing problems: the causes of sickness or natural disasters, for

---

1. "To the Honorable Men of the World," *The Evening and the Morning Star* 1, no. 3 (August 1832): 21.

2. Dallin H. Oaks, "Joseph Smith in a Personal World," *BYU Studies* 44, no. 4 (2005): 167.

example. They are good at explaining how some things happen but incapable of explaining ultimately why they happen. They are powerless to verify or disprove Joseph Smith's testimony of a heavenly vision. People who think in these ways alone can *assume,* as one scholar did, that "the revelation to Moses as recorded in the OT [Old Testament] can hardly be taken literally as an event in which the Divine handed over or dictated to Moses Ten Commandments," but how does he *know* that?[3] What is stated with such scholarly certainty as a foregone conclusion is nothing more than a personal opinion reflecting an assumption about what is possible.

Agnosticism, or not knowing, is another alternative. It is the conviction that ultimate things are unknowable. As with Joseph Smith's epistemology, agnosticism is based on personal experience, or lack thereof, with God. Agnostics know that they do not know ultimate things, and many agnostics assume that no one else knows either.

Surely there are other ways that people strive to know the answers to the questions our existence presents. Each leads to different answers. From among all these alternatives, Joseph Smith chose to be a seeker. To *seek* is to search or quest for the unknown. The *Oxford English Dictionary* defines *seek* as "to approach or draw near to (God) in prayer." It defines a *seeker* as "a searcher, an explorer, one who endeavours to find something hidden or lost, as in *seeker after truth.*" Joseph Smith recognized that he lacked the ultimate knowledge of salvation. He desired it deeply. He thought, read, observed, analyzed, and finally

---

3. W. D. Davies, "Reflections on the Mormon 'Canon,'" *Harvard Theological Review* 79 (January 1986): 64n41.

prayed to find it. He worked hard for it. He struggled. Seeking is active, not passive. Seeking is not spiritual *or* intellectual. Seeking is spiritual *and* intellectual. Seeking requires the whole soul, all of one's faculties. Seeking is the investment of one's best brainwork, spiritual sensitivities, moral judgments, and emotional vulnerabilities. Seeking is humble. Seeking is hard. And seeking is ultimately satisfying.

Assuming is the enemy of seeking. The word *assume* has many definitions. The ones meant here are to pretend to possess, to put forth claims or pretensions, to take for granted as the basis of argument or action, to suppose. To assume is to avoid the hard work of seeking. Assumptions are not knowledge, but often those who hold them do not discern the difference. At best, assumptions are hypotheses—the beginning, not the end, of knowledge. At worst, assumptions masquerade as knowledge, pacifying those who hold them and keeping them from seeking. Assumptions thus prevent us from ultimate knowing. Assuming is intellectually and spiritually lazy. It is arrogant. It is easy. And, though temporarily attractive, it is ultimately unsatisfying and can be spiritually devastating.

> *And as all have not faith, seek ye diligently and teach one another words of wisdom; yea, seek ye out of the best books words of wisdom; seek learning, even by study and also by faith.*
> DOCTRINE & COVENANTS 88:118.

Seeking is a scriptural imperative, a commandment. Over and over the scriptures enjoin us to seek. A single verse, Doctrine and Covenants 88:118, commands three times that we should seek. It tells us why to seek: because we lack faith. It tells us what to seek: learning. It tells us where to seek: out of the best books. It tells us how to seek: diligently, as well as by study and also by faith. Joseph repeated this verse in the dedication of the house of the Lord in Kirtland, Ohio, and prayed that the Saints would act on it (D&C 109:7, 14). Similar instructions pervade all of the scriptures. Sometimes the scriptures command us to seek with a modifying adverb, as in seek *diligently,* or seek *earnestly* (D&C 46:6; 88:118). Sometimes they tell us what to seek (Amos 5:4–6, 14; D&C 6:6; 11:7, 21; 25:10; 46:8; 88:118; Jacob 2:18). Sometimes they tell us what *not* to seek (D&C 6:7; 11:7; 22:4; 66:10; Jacob 4:10; Alma 39:14). Some of the most beautiful passages are the ones that attach specific promises to seeking. "Seek the Lord, and ye shall live," says one (Amos 5:6), an if-then formulation reiterated in the Doctrine and Covenants: "Seek the face of the Lord always, that in patience ye may possess your souls, and ye shall have eternal life" (101:38; see also 11:23; 88:83). Seeking is the means to knowing God, which is to have eternal life (John 17:3). We could profitably spend a long time studying the scriptures that teach us to seek; on the other hand, a computer search for the word *assume* reports no instances of *assume* in the scriptures.

This philosophical and dictionary work has everything to do with Joseph Smith's first vision. Individuals concerned about knowing whether Joseph told the truth approach the issue either as seekers or as assumers. Seekers come to the quest open-minded and open-hearted, desiring to know whether and in what ways Joseph's testimony is true and willing to use any means—spiritual *and* intellectual—to gain that knowledge. Assumers, whether believing or unbelieving, presuppose that they have knowledge. What more is there for them to learn? They are narrow-minded, closed to at least some of the possible means of knowing. Rather than hold assumptions tentatively and subject them to testing and verification, assumers have already arrived at the conclusion. They do not want to know any more. They do not seek the historical record, the rich documentation of the vision, asking of it all it can reveal to them. Rather, they tell it what it can say. They pick and choose bits that match their assumptions, their prejudices.

The historical method is the means that seekers can use to gain knowledge of the accounts of Joseph's vision. This disciplined way of thinking identifies and sorts different kinds of information. It seeks knowledge of the past from those who experienced it. It discerns the difference between historical facts and interpretations of those facts or opinions about them. In this way of thinking, historical (notice the qualifying adjective) facts are pieces of knowledge about the past that can be verified. In other words, disciplined historians recognize that their knowledge of the past is severely limited. They are careful to convey facts that any other historian could verify. And disciplined historians recognize, and help others to recognize, when they are interpreting facts or expressing opinion.

Disciplined historians build their interpretations of the past on historical facts. Practitioners of the historical method could think of their reconstruction of the past as if it were a house of cards. They can confidently construct only a single level on a firm, factual foundation. To build any higher increases exponentially the likelihood of error. Reliable historians do not, therefore, interpret far beyond what they *know*. And they clearly communicate what they know and how they know it. In that sense, Joseph Smith was a good historian. His autobiographies are strikingly straightforward, factual, and richly descriptive of his vision as he experienced it at the time and as he experienced it again and again through recollections and retellings over time.

Consider the following historical facts:

- Joseph Smith Jr., son of Lucy Mack and Joseph Smith Sr., was born in Vermont in 1805.
- Several documents created by Joseph Smith and his associates declare that he experienced a vision.
- These documents were written in the 1830s and 1840s.

These are historical truths that can be verified using the historical method. Notice, however, how little these facts actually communicate. The historical method is limited. It can tell us whether Joseph Smith was born in Vermont in 1805 but not whether he was called by God to be a prophet. It can show us several documents that testify that Joseph envisioned heavenly beings but cannot tell us whether the testimony is true or false. It can prove that the documents were written in the 1830s and 40s but not whether they accurately represent Joseph's experience in the grove. The historical facts do not prove or disprove whether Joseph experienced a vision, and any historian or Internet site saying otherwise is only expressing an opinion.

Seekers need the historical method to aid their quest, but it will ultimately fail to fulfill their desire to know whether

# SEEKING, ASSUMING, AND KNOWING

*Sacred Grove, Manchester, Ontario County, New York.
Photograph by George Edward Anderson, 1907.*

Joseph told the truth. Those who decide to seek by faith as well as by study incorporate the spiritual senses and ways of knowing into their method. This combination of seeking by study and by faith enables seekers to discern whether Joseph's accounts tell the truth. The foremost historians of the first vision are seekers of the study *and* faith variety. They are disciplined practitioners of the historical method who were trained in respected universities. By contrast, people who go from belief to unbelief when they confront the historical documents are comparatively ignorant of the historical method. Having visited with many of them, I believe that they are generally sincere but poorly informed souls who assumed they were well-informed and then found themselves in a crisis of faith when they encountered evidence that overturned their assumptions. They did not practice a disciplined method. They did not seek by diligent, systematic study along with exercising faith. Googling is not a synonym for seeking. The hard work of simultaneously seeking by study and by faith prevents this problem. After all the hard work of studying Joseph's testimony, and before and during as well, those who seek by study and by faith pray for confirmation of Joseph's testimony from God himself.

Joseph was a seeker. He created historical documents that testify that he experienced a heavenly vision. In doing so, he left us evidence of his effective epistemology, his way of knowing. By richly documenting his first vision, Joseph gave us his testimony to verify and he illustrated how it could be done.

CHAPTER 2

# Joseph Smith's Family and Culture

In January 1796 Lucy Mack married Joseph Smith, the second son of Asael and Mary Duty Smith. They began their new life together in a world quite different from that of their parents'. Between Joseph's birth in 1771 and Lucy's in 1775, a skirmish began in Lexington, Massachusetts, not far from the birthplace of either. This clash between colonial militiamen and British regulars sparked the American Revolution, which consumed the following seven years. Joseph's father, Asael Smith, enlisted as a soldier in the American army. The war ended in Joseph's ninth year when the American army, led by General George Washington, defeated the British with help from French allies.

During Joseph's and Lucy's childhood, Washington and others wrote a document that invented a new country: the United States of America. The Constitution indicated that the government would not control the church and the church would not control the government. For perhaps the first time in history, the people of a nation were free to choose any church or no church at all. Asael Smith rejoiced, "[God] has conducted us through a glorious revolution and has brought us into the promised land of peace and liberty." Like other Christians of his era, he was sure that the new nation would play a key role in God's plans, as foretold by prophecy. He further believed that one of his own descendants would be instrumental in the unfolding drama.[1]

Beginning in 1799, three years after Joseph Smith and Lucy Mack were married in Tunbridge, Vermont, periodic and scattered religious revivals marked the beginning of an intense period of spiritual awakening. The newly created American nation seemed to foster spiritual needs that old approaches could not satisfy. New ministers with new methods made salvation an individual quest, and they took religion to the people, especially on the frontier. Preaching in the open air, these passionate ministers made every individual responsible to experience religious rebirth. The response was phenomenal, especially in western New York, the home of one-third of the approximately six thousand American converts to Presbyterianism in 1820.[2] Baptist churches similarly boomed.[3] Methodism expanded impressively as traveling preachers blazed across the countryside like wildfire and gathered converts.[4]

Much was at stake in the churches' competitive quest for

---

1. Richard L. Anderson, *Joseph Smith's New England Heritage*, rev. ed. (Salt Lake City: Deseret Book; Provo, Utah: Brigham Young University Press, 2003), 132; spelling standardized.
2. Milton V. Backman Jr., "Awakenings in the Burned-Over District: New Light on the Historical Setting of the First Vision," *BYU Studies* 9, no 3 (Spring 1969): 317.
3. Jon Butler, *Awash in a Sea of Faith: Christianizing the American People* (Cambridge: Harvard University Press, 1990), 268–69; Backman, "Awakenings in the Burned-Over District," 314–15, 318.
4. John H. Wigger, *Taking Heaven by Storm* (Oxford: Oxford University Press, 1998), 3–6.

souls. The most pressing issue was the role of individual choice in one's own salvation. Calvinists often imagined God as an arbitrary, fierce sovereign, and they envisioned humankind, as a result of the Fall, as totally depraved sinners powerless to choose salvation through Christ. In Jonathan Edwards's memorable words, we are "boundless" in our "corruption," living perpetually "beneath the black clouds of God's wrath."[5] The Savior Jesus Christ atoned for the few he had mysteriously predestined to salvation but would justifiably damn most.

This idea of a limited atonement made God "worse than the devil . . . more false, more cruel, more unjust," wrote John Wesley, the founder of Methodism.[6] Wesley rejected Calvinism in favor of Arminian theology—the doctrines of Dutch theologian Jacob Arminius—who responded to Calvinism with a different interpretation of the Bible. Arminius, and later Wesley, believed mankind was fallen and predisposed to sin but not totally depraved. Rather, Arminians believed that God's grace endowed individuals with the ability to choose Christ and that he was mighty to save all who chose to be saved. New England Puritans had brought their Calvinist ideas to America; they founded the Congregational church. They were followed across the Atlantic by fellow Calvinists in Presbyterian and Reformed churches. Methodists came later with their Arminian doctrine.

---

5. Jonathan Edwards, "Sinners in the Hands of an Angry God," in John E. Smith, Harry S. Stout, and Kenneth P. Minkema, eds., *A Jonathan Edwards Reader* (New Haven: Yale University Press, 2003), 96.

6. John Wesley, "Sermon 128—Free Grace," http://www.umcmission.org/Find-Resources/Global-Worship-and-Spiritual-Growth/John-Wesley-Sermons/Sermon-128-Free-Grace, accessed 10 October 2012.

*This image is thought to be Lucy Mack Smith in her later years.*

Baptists split, meanwhile, some tending one way and some the other.

Unlike their parents and grandparents who were married in the Congregational church, Joseph and Lucy Mack Smith were married by a justice of the peace. Neither of them belonged to a church, and in that they were not unusual. By the time of their marriage, the Revolution had reshaped not only their political fortunes but also their religious ones. Optimistic ideas of human liberty led people to think of themselves as less sinful and with more innate potential than Congregational ministers had long taught. Such ideas caught hold in an environment ripe with unprecedented political, economic, and cultural freedom. Some people became confident that they could choose to follow Christ and elect to be saved rather than hoping and waiting for him to elect them. Universalists went even further, believing a generous God would redeem mankind without exceptions. And yet others, convinced they were not victims of Adam's fall, decided they did not need Jesus Christ at all. Believers labeled this attitude "infidelity" and worried that it might sweep the nation. Ministers grew concerned that frontiers and economic forces were pulling Americans away from established churches and determined to curb "the tide of infidelity which was setting in with so strong a current."[7]

Amidst these contrasting opinions, Asael Smith and his son Joseph came to believe that God was much more loving than they had been taught in church. They rejected the Calvinist idea of limited atonement. "Jesus Christ," Asael told his family, "can as well save all, as any." This way of thinking became known as Universalism, and Asael and his son Joseph organized a Universalist Society the year after Joseph and Lucy were married, while other churches continued their unprecedented growth.[8]

As children began to bless their home, Joseph and Lucy were challenged to make their way economically. Providing for their family became as problematic as choosing their faith in a new religious landscape. Joseph and Lucy felt pressed to provide their children with both faith and food. Even so, at this point their future looked bright. Asael gave Joseph ownership of a farm, and Lucy's brother Stephen gave her one thousand dollars as a dowry. Wheat prices were good that year, and although the Smith's first child, a son, died at birth, two fine sons followed shortly—Alvin in 1799 and Hyrum in 1801. Sophronia, their first daughter, came next in 1803. After a few years in Tunbridge, the young family moved to nearby

---

7. James H. Hotchkin, *A History of the Purchase and Settlement of Western New York, and the Rise, Progress, and Present State of the Presbyterian Church in That Section* (New York: M. W. Dodd, 1848), 74.

8. Anderson, *Joseph Smith's New England Heritage,* 162; spelling and capitalization standardized; see also 133–35.

Randolph, where Joseph and Lucy opened a store in the growing town. While working there, Joseph and Lucy risked their fortune on a shipment of ginseng root, an herb that grew wild in the Vermont hills and sold for huge profits in China. Joseph and Lucy were cheated by the man they trusted to make the delivery, and they lost everything. Debts swallowed the farm and the money from Lucy's dowry. Penniless and propertyless, the Smiths were faced with a dim future.

For the next several years, Joseph and Lucy moved from farm to farm as their family grew. Joseph Jr. was born in 1805, Samuel in 1808, Ephraim (who lived only a few days) in 1810, William in 1811, Katharine in 1813, Don Carlos in 1816 and Lucy in 1821.

Two decades earlier, about 1802, a severe fever had attacked Lucy. The doctors gave up hope for her life, and she fearfully faced death. "I am not prepared to die, for I do not know the ways of Christ," she fretted, "and it seemed to me as though there was a dark and lonely chasm between myself and Christ that I dared not attempt to cross." Lucy pleaded for direction and "covenanted with God that if he would let me live, I would endeavor to get that religion that would enable me to serve him right, whether it was in the Bible or wherever it might be found." From then on, Lucy wrote, religion "occupied my mind entirely."[9]

She was not alone. Among the thousands attracted to Methodism was a schoolteacher, nineteen-year-old George Lane, a man who was later said to have contributed to Joseph

---

9. Lucy Mack Smith, *History of Joseph Smith by His Mother,* ed. Scot Facer Proctor and Maurine Jensen Proctor (Salt Lake City: Bookcraft, 1996), 47–50.

Smith Jr.'s spiritual awakening. In 1803 George "was absent from the school a few days, and when he returned he told his scholars that he had experienced religion, and exhorted them and prayed with them, and a great revival broke out immediately."[10] Lane left his school in 1804 and began to climb the ranks of the Methodist ministry, putting in long preaching tours and proving himself both diligent and gifted, until he was physically weakened and opted for an easier career minding a store before being beckoned back into the ministry.

Meanwhile, the opportunities and pressures of the new nation sent the Smiths, along with many others, seeking power to secure both temporal and spiritual salvation. In 1816 they left New England and Lucy's mother for the bustling economic and religious scene of Palmyra, New York. There the Smith family found a religious revival firing the souls of their new neighbors. The number of local Baptists increased in spurts. The number of Palmyra's Presbyterians doubled, and a new congregation formed between the Smiths' arrival in 1816 and their move south of town about two years later; in 1819 there were more local Presbyterian converts than in any previous year. Methodists built a new meetinghouse in 1821.[11]

Joseph and Lucy Smith and their large family found frontier prices in this environment. Land was cheap, but food and supplies were expensive. They "counseled together as to what course it was best to take." According to Lucy, they agreed

---

10. George Peck, *Early Methodism within the Bounds of Old Genesee Conference from 1788 to 1828; or, The First Forty Years of Wesleyan Evangelism in Northern Pennsylvania, Central and Western New York, and Canada* (New York: Carlton and Porter, 1860), 449.
11. Richard L. Bushman, *Joseph Smith and the Beginnings of Mormonism* (Urbana: University of Illinois Press, 1984), 53.

that each able family member would "apply all our energies together and endeavor to obtain a piece of land."[12] High wages drew Joseph Sr. with his two eldest sons, Alvin and Hyrum, to odd jobs until they had enough to pursue the increasingly American dream of owning land—the means of their own prosperity. Lucy painted rugs and tablecloths to supply the family's daily needs. Joseph Jr., who grew from about age ten to twelve while his family lived in Palmyra, wrote of his family's "indigent circumstances" in this era and of being "obliged to labour hard for the support of a large Family."[13] But that hard work in the frontier economy paid off; the Smiths were able to contract for a wooded lot in Manchester, New York, south of Palmyra.[14]

In Manchester they built a small log home, planted an orchard, produced sugar from their maple trees, and began clearing the land. Lucy said it was "not long until we had thirty acres ready for cultivation," representing a remarkable amount of work.[15] Joseph labored along with the rest of his family. According to one secondhand account, in seeking a secluded spot for his most momentous prayer, Joseph "went out into the woods where my father had a clearing, and went to the stump where I had stuck my axe."[16]

But in the meantime the Smith family's economic insecurities were compounded by spiritual ones. Joseph Sr. became

---

12. Smith, *History of Joseph Smith*, 86.
13. Dean C. Jessee, ed., "The Early Accounts of Joseph Smith's First Vision," *BYU Studies* 9 (Spring 1969): 279.
14. Bushman, *Beginnings of Mormonism*, 46.
15. Smith, *History of Joseph Smith*, 86–88; Bushman, *Beginnings of Mormonism*, 48.
16. Milton V. Backman Jr., *Joseph Smith's First Vision* (Salt Lake City: Bookcraft, 1970), 176.

aloof from all formal denominations, and though both he and Lucy were sincere believers, neither found spiritual rest in the competing congregations of Presbyterians, Methodists, Quakers, and Baptists. Lucy dreamed of finding economic and spiritual security, both of which seemed to elude her and her family. A few years earlier in New England, Lucy had suffered with her children through a devastating typhoid epidemic. She had earlier lost two of her sisters to death and later left her aging mother in New England. Meanwhile she had made her own death-bed covenant to get religion if God would preserve her life, which he had. She had tried Presbyterianism, "but all was emptiness," thence Methodism, but Joseph Sr. "had so little faith in the doctrine taught by them." His lack of interest, together with pressure from her father-in-law, Asael, to leave Methodism alone, left Lucy "very much hurt." She retired to a nearby grove of wild cherry trees and prayed to the Lord to soften her husband's heart. Later Lucy dreamed of two trees, one of which was pliant and lively, the other unbending. She came to understand that the flexible tree represented her husband, who would hear and receive the "pure and undefiled gospel of the Son of God" at a future time.[17] The experience brought Lucy a measure of comfort amidst her ongoing quest for spiritual security and peace.

Joseph Smith Sr.'s anxieties were also manifest in dreams. In one he was footsore and weary. A guide showed him to a beautiful flower garden in which he was renewed. "I then asked my guide the meaning of all this," Lucy remembered

---

17. Smith, *History of Joseph Smith*, 47–50, 58–60.

him saying, "but I awoke before I received an answer." In the second dream Father Smith walked wearily to what seemed like final judgment; he arrived too late and was denied admission. "I found that my flesh was perishing," Lucy quoted him as saying. "I continued to pray, still my flesh withered away upon my bones. I was in a state of almost total despair." At that point the doorkeeper questioned whether he had met all the requirements for admission, to which he replied, "All that was in my power to do." He was told that mercy could take effect only after justice was satisfied, so he cried out in soulful agony for forgiveness in the name of Jesus Christ. His strength returned, and the door opened, "but on entering," he reported, "I awoke." In a third dream Lucy dated to 1819, Joseph Sr. dreamed he met a peddler who promised to tell him the one thing he lacked to secure his salvation. He "sprang to get some paper" but awoke in the excitement.[18]

Such anxious seeking in a mother and father while raising a large family in a culture confounded by choices between this church or that one created a seeking son named for his father—Joseph Smith Jr.

---

18. Smith, *History of Joseph Smith,* 89–90, 94.

CHAPTER 3

# "The Lord Opened the Heavens upon Me"

---

Joseph Smith Jr. matured under the care of what he called "goodly Parents who spared no pains" to teach him Christian principles. But no one in the Smith household could escape the tensions and anxieties inherent in their relentless quest for security in an insecure world. Joseph wrote that in the aftermath of the 1816–17 Palmyra-area revival, "at about the age of twelve my mind become seriously imprest with regard to the all importent concerns for the welfare of my immortal soul."[1] The recurrent revivals put the urgent question, "What must I do to be saved?" foremost in his mind. The question became inescapable even as its answer remained elusive. "Being wrought up in my mind, respecting the subject of religion," Joseph explained, "and looking at the different systems . . . I knew not who was right or who was wrong and I considered it of the first importance that I should be right in matters that involve eternal consequences."[2] He wrote, "[I became] exceedingly distressed for I become convicted of my sins and by searching

---

1. See Joseph's 1832 account in chapter 4.
2. See Joseph's 9 November 1835 account in chapter 4.

*Reverend George Lane (1784–1859), engraved portrait from* Methodist Magazine, *April 1826.*

the scriptures I found that mankind did not come unto the Lord but that they had apostatised from the true and living faith and there was no society or denomination that built upon the gospel of Jesus Christ as recorded in the new testament and I felt to mourn for my own sins and for the sins of the world."[3]

An 1818 camp meeting in the hills above Wilkes-Barre, Pennsylvania, reminded George Lane how exciting it felt to experience religion and how rewarding it was to lead willing souls to the Savior. After an extended absence, he returned to the ministry of the Methodist Episcopal church. On Thursday, 1 July 1819, he attended the annual Genesee conference, convened in Vienna (now Phelps), New York, a half-day's walk from the Smith family farm.[4] With more than one hundred ministers

---

3. See Joseph's 1832 account in chapter 4.
4. Larry C. Porter, "Reverend George Lane—Good 'Gifts,' Much 'Grace,' Marked 'Usefulness,'" *BYU Studies* 9:3 (Spring 1969): 328.

gathered from the whole region, the area pulsed with "unusual excitement on the subject of religion."[5] One participant described the week-long event as a "religious cyclone which swept over the whole region"; Joseph Smith may have been in the eye of the storm.[6] An unfriendly acquaintance reported that Joseph caught a "spark of Methodism in the camp meeting, away down in the woods, on the Vienna road."[7] Reverend Lane may have especially influenced Joseph in this setting. None of Joseph's known accounts say so, but Oliver Cowdery thought Lane influenced Joseph, and Joseph's younger brother William recalled that Lane "preached a sermon on 'What church shall I join?' And the burden of his discourse was to ask God, using as a text, 'If any man lack wisdom let him ask of God who giveth to all men liberally.'"[8] Whether prompted by a preacher or not, the idea that he might exert himself to seek and thereby find a path to salvation led Joseph to prefer the Arminian doctrine of Methodism over the Calvinist doctrine of the Presbyterians. He felt partial toward the Methodists and wanted to join them, but he lacked the experience to be sure which doctrine was right. Joseph later told friends that during one Methodist meeting, "he wanted to feel and shout like the rest but could feel

---

5. See Joseph's 1838 account in chapter 4.
6. M. P. Blakeslee, Notes for a History of Methodism in Phelps, 1886, p. 78, Manuscript, L. Tom Perry Special Collections, Harold B. Lee Library, Brigham Young University, Provo, Utah.
7. Orsamus Turner, *History of the Pioneer Settlement of Phelps and Gorham's Purchase* (Rochester: William Alling, 1852), 214.
8. "Statement of William Smith, Concerning Joseph, the Prophet," *Deseret Evening News*, 20 January 1894, 11; quoted in Porter, "Reverend George Lane," 338.

nothing."⁹ Yet he was "greatly excited, the cry and tumult were so great and incessant."¹⁰

It was, Joseph wrote, "during this time of great excitement" that his religious concerns became a crisis. He wondered in his head whether the churches were "all wrong together" but resisted letting the awful thought enter his heart. At the same time, he experienced "confusion," "extreme difficulties," and "great uneasiness" caused by his sense of guilt for sins in the midst of a bewildering "war of words and tumult of opinions" about which church could furnish him with forgiveness.¹¹ "This was a grief to my Soul," Joseph said of the disparity he found between the doctrines taught by the various churches and the Bible.¹² Indeed, the Bible was both the battleground of this war and its greatest casualty, "for the teachers of religion of the different sects understood the same passages of scripture so differently as to destroy all confidence in settling the question by an appeal to the Bible." Yet it was the Bible's God to whom Joseph successfully appealed. He had listened over and over as religious partisans wielded the Bible as a weapon, "endeavoring to establish their own tenets and disprove all others." Now, perhaps prompted by the Reverend Lane, Joseph approached the Bible privately, quietly—more as a living word than a dead law—and it spoke to his seeking soul.¹³

He said he was "laboring under the extreme difficulties

---

9. See Alexander Neibaur's secondary account of the vision in chapter 4.
10. See Joseph's 1838 account in chapter 4.
11. See Joseph's 1838 account in chapter 4.
12. See Joseph's 1832 account in chapter 4.
13. See Joseph's 1838 account in chapter 4.

## "THE LORD OPENED THE HEAVENS UPON ME"

caused by the contests of these parties of religionists" when he read James 1:5: "If any of you lack wisdom, let him ask of God, that giveth to all men liberally, and upbraideth not; and it shall be given him." The passage made a permanent impression, sinking powerfully into Joseph's consciousness. "I reflected on it again and again," Joseph said, "knowing that if any person needed wisdom from God, I did; for how to act I did not know, and unless I could get more wisdom than I then had, I would never know." The biblical invitation to receive revelation moved Joseph deeply. "Never did any passage of scripture come with more power to the heart of man than this did at this time to mine. It seemed to enter with great force into every feeling of my heart. I reflected on it again and again, knowing that if any person needed wisdom from God, I did."[14]

On a clear spring morning in 1820, Joseph left his home to seek seclusion in the woods because he had determined to pray vocally for the first time in his life. He knelt but was overcome by some unseen power. Tongue-tied and enveloped by thick darkness, Joseph felt doomed. He had gone to the woods to test whether he could choose salvation and to learn whether his desires mattered to God. Did anyone but God have power in the universe? Did Joseph? He learned quickly of "the power of [an] enemy which had seized upon me," an astonishing "power of some actual being from the unseen world, who had such marvelous power as I had never before felt in any being." At the very moment when he had to choose whether or not he would succumb to that power, Joseph exerted what he

---

14. See Joseph's 1838 account in chapter 4.

called "all my powers to call upon God to deliver me out of the power of this enemy." And just at that moment Joseph became conscious of a heavenly light, brighter than the sun, descending upon him and delivering him from the awful power. His prayer had opened heaven and invoked power that vanquished the most potent opposing force Joseph had ever experienced.[15]

Joseph had gone to the grove to find forgiveness, and he emphasized his success in that quest when he wrote his first, rough autobiography in 1832: "I was filled with the spirit of god and the <Lord> opened the heavens upon me and I saw the Lord and he spake unto me saying Joseph <my son> thy sins are forgiven thee." The Savior confirmed Joseph's observations that "the world lieth in sin" and that the existing churches had "turned asside from the gospel and keep not <my> commandments they draw near to me with their lips while their hearts are far from me."[16]

Joseph asked the heavenly beings which church was right. He had often wondered whether they were all wrong but had kept the awful thought from entering his heart, as he said. "I was answered," Joseph reported, "that I must join none of them, for they were all wrong." Their creeds said that God was unknowable and incomprehensible, yet he was revealing himself to Joseph. The creeds said in the language of the philosophers that God was without body, parts, or passions. Joseph, on the other hand, saw and heard divine personages and said that their presence filled him with love. The Bible described

---

15. See Joseph's 1838 account in chapter 4.
16. See Joseph's 1832 account in chapter 4.

"THE LORD OPENED THE HEAVENS UPON ME"

*The Sacred Grove, near Palmyra, New York.
Photograph by George Edward Anderson, 1907.*

a powerful God, but Joseph soon discovered that the clergy with whom he communicated "den[ied] the power" that he experienced in the woods of western New York. Just days after the experience, Joseph related it to a Methodist preacher, who responded with surprising contempt, denying that God would commune with Joseph in such a way, "saying it was all of the devil, that there were no such things as visions or revelations in these days; that all such things had ceased with the apostles, and that there would never be any more of them." The response stung Joseph and taught him to keep the vision to himself. As he reflected in later years, he felt like the whole world was allied against him from that moment forward—ridiculing, reviling, persecuting, and leaving him without any friends but God. But in the meantime "my soul was filled with love," Joseph wrote with his own pen, "and for many days I could rejoice with great Joy and the Lord was with me but [I] could find none that would believe the hevnly vision nevertheless I pondered these things in my heart."[17]

Joseph Smith the seeker had found what he "most desired." He had "retired to the silent grove and there bowed down before the Lord" in faith, expecting that he could ask and receive, knock and have the door opened, seek and find.[18] He "had found the testimony of James to be true—that a man who lacked wisdom might ask of God, and obtain."[19] The answer to his prayerful quest was not the experience the revival preachers encouraged or that Joseph fully expected. There were no "shouts of rejoicing," no bench to sit on while the faithful prayed for him to get religion, no "deep tones of the preacher."[20] There was just Joseph in what he called the "wilderness," acting on the Bible's oft-repeated invitation to revelation: ask and receive.[21]

---

17. See Joseph's 1832 account in chapter 4.
18. See Joseph's 9 November 1835 account in chapter 4.
19. See Joseph's 1838 account in chapter 4.
20. *Minutes of the Annual Conferences,* 1860, p. 40; quoted in Porter, "Reverend George Lane," 325.
21. See Joseph's 1832 account in chapter 4.

CHAPTER 4

# A Well-Documented Theophany

Joseph Smith's first vision may be the best documented theophany in history. In the 1830s and 1840s Joseph wrote or caused scribes to write five known accounts declaring that the Lord opened the heavens upon him. Four of these five documents were later copied at least once, sometimes more, resulting in revisions each time. Five other known writers documented the event during Joseph's lifetime. Scholars would be thrilled to have that much primary and secondary documentation of Moses' encounter at the burning bush, Isaiah's vision of the heavenly temple, or Paul's experience on the road to Damascus.

Joseph Smith worked hard to document his experience in the grove, and scholars have worked hard to raise awareness of his several accounts. The Church and various scholars have published and publicized these documents repeatedly for half a century now. Images of the documents containing the primary accounts are in the Selected Collections from the Archives of The Church of Jesus Christ of Latter-day Saints. The accounts are being published again and put online as part of the Joseph Smith Papers Project (josephsmithpapers.org). Even so, they are little known by most Latter-day Saints and others. Strangely, some believers do not want to know the plentiful historical record. They can hardly be troubled with Joseph's efforts to capture his sublime experience. Some critics, meanwhile, assert that the documentary richness shows Joseph to be a fraud. But seekers are not satisfied with either of these approaches. They thirst for all the evidence and examine it for themselves. They read, remember, and ponder Joseph's descriptions. They seek understanding and verification. This presentation of the accounts is for them.

The first vision accounts were created in specific historical settings that shape what they say and how they say it. Each of the accounts of Joseph Smith's first vision has its own history. Each was created in circumstances that determined how it was remembered and communicated and thus how it was transmitted to us. Each account has gaps and omissions. Each adds detail and richness.

### Primary Accounts of Joseph Smith's First Vision

- 1832—autobiography written on the first pages of a book used by Joseph Smith to record letters he sent and received
- 1835 (November 9)—entry in Joseph Smith's journal by his scribe, reporting Joseph's account of the vision to a visitor; reproduced in 1834–36 history
- 1835 (November 14)—entry in Joseph Smith's journal by his scribe, reporting Joseph's account of the vision to Erastus Holmes; reproduced in 1834–36 history
- 1838—account scribed by George Robinson and copied into Joseph's History by James Mulholland and later revised, presumably by Joseph, and copied again by Howard Coray

about 1841; published in the *Times and Seasons* newspaper on March 15, 1842; redacted by Willard Richards later that year; later excerpted in the Pearl of Great Price.

- 1842—Joseph Smith letter to John Wentworth, published in the *Times and Seasons* newspaper on March 1, 1842; reproduced in 1843 for Israel Daniel Rupp's *An Original History of the Religious Denominations at Present Existing in the United States.*

---

## 1832 Account

Joseph's 1832 autobiography is the least polished of all his accounts. Here, with his own pen for much of the document, he poured his experience onto the pages, reflecting as nearly as possible what God's condescending visit meant to Joseph's sinful fourteen-year-old self. Later accounts are more conscious of the vision's significance for all mankind, but none surpasses this earliest known account at revealing what it meant personally to young Joseph Smith.

This 1832 account is part of Joseph's earliest autobiography, a rough, six-page statement of epic themes expressed in what Joseph called a "crooked broken scattered and imperfect Language."[1] It declares, "A History of the life of Joseph Smith Jr. an account of his marvilous experience and of all the mighty acts which he doeth in the name of Jesus Ch[r]ist the son of the living God of whom he beareth record and also an account of

---

1. Joseph Smith to William W. Phelps, 27 November 1832, Church History Library, The Church of Jesus Christ of Latter-day Saints, Salt Lake City, Utah; hereafter cited as Church History Library. Available online at http://josephsmithpapers.org/paperSummary/letter-to-william-w-phelps-27-november-1832.

the rise of the church of Christ in the eve of time according as the Lord brough<t> forth and established by his hand."

Joseph Smith and Frederick Williams wrote this document in 1832, probably between July and November. Joseph's first counselor, Sidney Rigdon, declared on July 5 that year, among Saints in Kirtland, Ohio, that authority had been taken from the Church. When Joseph addressed the Saints in Kirtland on 8 July, he confiscated President Rigdon's preaching license and asserted, "I myself hold the Keys of this last dispensation and I forever will hold them in time and in eternity."[2] Soon after, Frederick G. Williams, Joseph's second counselor, assumed President Rigdon's role as Joseph's scribe.[3] Williams then began to pen Joseph's autobiography until, partway down the first page, Joseph picked up the pen himself and wrote much of the rest.

### Timeline of Publications of the First Vision Accounts

Dean C. Jessee, one of the leading scholars of Joseph Smith's papers, is a pioneer in publishing lesser known accounts of the first vision. When asked about the surprise some people experience when they learn there are multiple accounts, Dean smiled and gently replied, "I think people who are surprised today that there are different accounts are used to the one that's been canonized for so long, the one we constantly refer to. People would not be surprised if they were more inclined to read. All of the accounts have been

---

2. Lucy Mack Smith, *Lucy's Book: A Critical Edition of Lucy Mack Smith's Family Memoir*, ed. Lavina Fielding Anderson (Salt Lake City: Signature Books, 2001), 560–63.
3. Frederick G. Williams Papers, 1834–1842, MS 782, folder 1, item 6, Church History Library. Joseph Smith began his 31 July 1832 letter to William Phelps: "I sit down to dictate for Broth Frederick to write." Retained copy in handwriting of Frederick G. Williams, Church History Library.

available for years and years, published in various places. If people are interested in finding and learning, they can certainly do it."[4]

Selected list of accounts published in the twentieth and early twenty-first centuries:

- 1965. Paul R. Cheesman, "An Analysis of the Accounts Relating to Joseph Smith's Early Visions," master's thesis, Brigham Young University, 1965, especially pages 126–32.
- 1969. Dean C. Jessee, "The Early Accounts of Joseph Smith's First Vision," *BYU Studies* 9:3 (1969): 275–94.
- 1970. James B. Allen, "Eight Contemporary Accounts of Joseph Smith's First Vision—What Do We Learn from Them," *Improvement Era* 73 (April 1970): 4–13.
- 1971, 1980. Milton V. Backman Jr., *Joseph Smith's First Vision* (Salt Lake City: Bookcraft), 155–81.
- 1985. Milton V. Backman Jr., "Joseph Smith's Recitals of the First Vision," *Ensign,* January 1985, 8–17.
- 1996. Richard L. Anderson, "Joseph Smith's Testimony of the First Vision," *Ensign,* April 1996, 10–21.
- 2002. Dean C. Jessee, ed., *Personal Writings of Joseph Smith,* rev. ed. (Salt Lake City: Deseret Book and Provo, Utah: Brigham Young University Press, 2002) and *Papers of Joseph Smith,* 2 vols. (Salt Lake City: Deseret Book, 1989–1992), 9–248.
- 2005. John W. Welch, ed., *Opening the Heavens: Accounts of Divine Manifestations, 1820–1844* (Provo: Brigham Young University Press, 2005), 1–76.
- 2008. Dean C. Jessee, Mark Ashurst-McGee, and Richard L. Jensen, eds., *Journals, Volume 1: 1832–1839,* vol. 1 of the Journals series of The Joseph Smith Papers, edited by Dean C.

---

4. Dean C. Jessee, interview by Samuel Dodge, 27 July 2009, Provo, Utah; transcription in possession of the author.

Jessee, Ronald K. Esplin, and Richard Lyman Bushman (Salt Lake City: Church Historian's Press, 2008).

- 2012. Karen Lynn Davidson, David J. Whittaker, Mark Ashurst-McGee, and Richard L. Jensen, eds., *Histories, 1832–1844*, vol. 1 of the Histories series of *The Joseph Smith Papers*, edited by Dean C. Jessee, Ronald K. Esplin, and Richard Lyman Bushman (Salt Lake City: Church Historian's Press, 2012).

---

This remarkable document is not dated, but the context in which it was written seems to include Joseph's 27 November 1832 revelation, now published as Doctrine and Covenants 85, which reaffirmed the need for the Saints "to keep a history" and to document "their manner of life, their faith, and works" (D&C 85:1–2).[5] Joseph bought his first diary the day that revelation came, and he spent the next day "reading and writing."[6] He also began to record letters in the same book that he used to record his autobiography. The first letter in that book is dated the same day as the revelation. In fact, the letter includes the text of the revelation that became Doctrine and Covenants 85. Joseph and Frederick wrote Joseph's autobiography on the six pages that immediately preceded the letter in the record book. It seems likely that Joseph wrote his autobiography at about

---

5. Joseph Smith to William W. Phelps, 27 November 1832, Church History Library, The Church of Jesus Christ of Latter-day Saints, Salt Lake City; hereafter cited as Church History Library. Available online at http://josephsmithpapers.org/paperSummary/letter-to-william-w-phelps-27-november-1832.

6. Dean C. Jessee, Mark Ashurst-McGee, Richard L. Jensen, eds., *Journals, 1832–1839*, vol. 1 of the Journals series of *The Joseph Smith Papers*, edited by Dean C. Jessee, Ronald K. Esplin, and Richard Lyman Bushman (Salt Lake City: Church Historian's Press, 2008); see entries for dates noted above.

the time he began keeping a diary and recording his letters because he took personally the revelation to keep a history that documented his faith, life, and works.

Joseph described a highly personalized experience in his earliest account (1832). Using the language of the revivals, he describes his consciousness of his sins and of his frustrating inability to find forgiveness in a church that matched the New Testament version. This account emphasizes the atonement of Christ and the personal redemption it offered Joseph. He wrote in his own hand of the joy and love he felt as a result of the vision, though he could find no one who believed him.

---

"I'll never forget when I put my head into that microfilm machine in the Church Historical Department, started it going, and saw Joseph Smith's handwriting. And as I read through that first account of the First Vision, there was a feeling that came over me that I don't think I'd ever experienced before and it's not quite like anything I've experienced since that said to me, 'This young man is telling the truth.' It was a powerful story. It was a handwritten story that didn't have very good grammar and no punctuation. There may have been one long, maybe two sentences in the whole thing. . . . But the power that was in it representing the feelings of a young man who is trying to put across how he felt . . . was just absolutely powerful to me."

—James B. Allen

---

Joseph Smith and Frederick Williams wrote this earliest known account a decade before some of Joseph's later accounts were published. The Church's historians brought this document across the plains to Utah and kept it in the Church Historian's Office, where it remained generally unknown to Latter-day Saints until Paul Cheesman published it in his master's thesis in 1965.[7] Bolded text below represents text written by Joseph Smith himself (see Plates 1–6).

## Transcription of 1832 Account

A History of the life of Joseph Smith Jr. an account of his marvilous experience and of all the mighty acts which he doeth in the name of Jesus Ch[r]ist the son of the living God of whom he beareth record and also an account of the rise of the church of Christ in the eve of time according as the Lord brough&lt;t&gt; forth and established by his hand &lt;firstly&gt; he receiving the testamony from on high seccondly the ministering of Angels thirdly the reception of the holy Priesthood by the ministering of Aangels to administer the letter of the Gospel— &lt;—the Law and Commandments as they were given unto him—&gt; and the ordinencs, forthly a confirmation and reception of the high Priesthood after the holy order of the son of the living God power and ordinence from on high to preach the Gospel in the administration and demonstration of the spirit **the Kees of the Kingdom of God confered upon him and the continuation of the blessings of God to him &c—I was born in the town of Charon [Sharon] in the &lt;State&gt; of Vermont North America on the twenty third day of December A.D. 1805 of goodly Parents who spared no paints instruct&lt;ing&gt; me in &lt;the&gt; christian religion at the age of about ten years my**

---

7. Paul R. Cheesman, "An Analysis of the Accounts Relating to Joseph Smith's Early Visions" (master's thesis, Brigham Young University, 1965), 126–32.

PLATE 1. *Joseph Smith's brief 1832 autobiography was written on the first few pages of his Letterbook 1. Photograph by Welden C. Andersen.*

Page 1

A History of the life of Joseph Smith Jr. an account of his marvilous experience and of all the mighty acts which he doeth in the name of Jesus Christ the son of the living God of whom he beareth record and also an account of the rise of the church of Christ in the eve of time according as the Lord brought forth and established by his hand firstly he receiving the testamony from on high seccondly the ministering of Angels thirdly the reception of the holy Priesthood by the ministring of Angels to administer the letter of the Gospel — the Law and commandments as they were given unto him— and the ordinances, forthly a confirmation and reception of the high Priesthood after the holy order of the son of the living God power and ordinence from on high to preach the Gospel in the administration and demonstration of the spirit the Kee of the Kingdom of God confered upon him and the continuation of the blessings of God to him &c

I was born in the town of Charon in the State of Vermont North America on the twenty third day of December AD 1805 of Goodly Parents who spared no pains to instructing me in the Christian religion at the age of about ten years my Father Joseph Smith Sinior moved to Palmyra Ontario County in the State of New York and being in indigent circumstances were obliged to labour hard for the support of a large Family having nine Children and as it required the exertions of all that were able to render any assistance for the support of the Family therefore we were deprived of the bennifit of an education suffice it to say I was merely instructed in reading and writing and the ground rules of Arithmatic which constuted my whole literary acquirements. At about the age of twelve years my mind become seriously imprest

PLATE 2. *Joseph Smith, Letterbook 1, page 1.*

with regard to the all important concerns for the welfare of my immortal Soul which led me to searching the Scriptures believing as I was taught, that they contained the word of God thus applying myself to them and my intimate acquaintance with those of different denominations led me to marvel exceedingly for I discovered that they did not adorn their profession by a holy walk and Godly conversation agreeable to what I found contained in that sacred depository this was a grief to my Soul thus from the age of twelve years to fifteen I pondered many things in my heart concerning the situation of the world of mankind the contentions and divions the wickeness and abominations and the darkness which pervaded the minds of mankind my mind become exceedingly distressed for I become convicted of my sins and by searching the Scriptures I found that mankind did not come unto the Lord but that they had apostatised from the true and liveing faith and there was no society or denomination that built upon the gospel of Jesus Christ as recorded in the new testament and I felt to mourn for my own sins and for the sins of the world for I learned in the Scriptures that God was the same yesterday to day and forever that he was no respecter to persons for he was God for I looked upon the sun the glorious luminary of the earth and also the moon rolling in their majesty through the heavens and also the stars shining in their courses and the earth also upon which I stood and the beast of the field and the fowls of heaven and the fish of the waters and also man walking forth upon the face of the earth in magesty and in the strength of beauty whose power and intiligence in governing the things which are so exceding great and marvilous even in the likeness of him who created them and when I considered upon these things my heart exclaimed well hath the wise man said it is a fool that saith in his heart there is no God my heart exclaimed all all these bear testimony and bespeak an omnipotent and omnipresent power a being who maketh Laws and decreeth and bindeth all things in their bounds who filleth Eternity who was and is and will be from all Eternity to Eternity and when I considered all these things and that that being seeketh such to worship him as worship him in spirit and in truth therefore I cried unto the Lord for mercy for there was none else to whom I could go and to obtain mercy and the Lord heard my cry in the wilderness and while in the attitude of calling upon the Lord a pillar of light above the brightness of the sun at noon day come down from above and rested upon me and I was filled with the spirit of God and the Lord opened the heavens upon me and I saw the Lord and he spake unto me saying Joseph my son thy sins are forgiven thee. go thy way walk in my statutes and keep my commandments behold I am the Lord of glory I was crucifyed for the world that all those who believe on my name may have Eternal life behold the world lieth in sin at this time and none doeth good no not one they have turned asside from the Gospel and keep not my commandments they draw near to me with their lips while their hearts are far from me and mine anger is kindling against the inhabitants of the earth to visit them acording to this ungodliness and to bring to pass that which hath been spoken by the mouth of the prophets and apostles behold and lo I come quickly as it written of me in the cloud clothed in the glory of my Father and my soul was filled with love and for many days I could rejoice with great joy and the Lord was with me but could find none that would believe the heavenly vision nevertheless I pondered these things in my heart about that time my mother but after many days

PLATE 4. *Joseph Smith, Letterbook 1, page 3.*

PLATE 5. Joseph Smith, Letterbook 1, page 3, detail. Insertion is in the handwriting of Frederick G. Williams.

PLATE 6. Frederick G. Williams.

PLATE 7. *Joseph Smith, 1835–1836 Journal, cover.*
*Photograph by Welden C. Andersen.*

I should think he is about 50 or 55 years old, tall and strait slender built of thin visage blue eyes, and fair complexion, he wore a sea-green frock coat, & pantaloons of the same, black fur hat with narrow brim, and while speaking, frequently shuts his eyes with a scowl on his countenance: I made some inquiry after his name but received no definite answer; we soon commenced talking upon the subject of religion, and after I had made some remarks concerning the bible I commenced giving him a relation of the circumstances connected with the coming forth of the book of Mormon, as follows— being wrought up in my mind, respecting the subject of religion and looking at the different systems taught the children of men, I knew not who was right or who was wrong and I considered it of the first importance that I should be right, in matters that involve eternal consequences; being thus perplexed in mind I retired to the silent grove and bowd down before the Lord, under a realizing sense that he had said (if the bible be true) ask and you shall receive knock and it shall be opened seek and you shall find and again, if any man lack wisdom let him ask of God who giveth to all men liberally and upbradeth not, information was what I most desired at this time, and with a fixed determination to obtain it, I called upon the Lord for the first time, in the place above stated or in other words I made a fruitless attempt to pray, my tongue seemed to be swolen in my mouth, so that I could not utter, I heard a noise behind me like some person walking towards me, I strove again to pray, but could not, the noise of walking seemed to draw nearer, I sprung up on my feet, and

24 and looked around, but saw no person or thing that was calculated to produce the noise of walking, I kneeled again my mouth was opened and my tongue liberated, and I called on the Lord in mighty prayer, a pillar of fire appeared above my head, it presently rested down upon me, and filled me with joy unspeakable, a personage appeared in the midst of this pillar of flame which was spread all around, and yet nothing consumed, another personage soon appeared like unto the first, he said unto me thy sins are forgiven thee, he testified unto me that Jesus Christ is the son of God; <and I saw many angels in this vision> I was about 14 years old when I received this first communication; When I was about 17 years old I saw another vision of angels, in the night season after I had retired to bed I had not been asleep, <when> but was meditating upon my past life and experience, I was very conscious that I had not kept the commandments, and I repented heartily for all my sins and transgression, and humbled myself before Him; <whose eyes are on all things> all at once the room was illuminated above the brightness of the sun an angel appeared before me, his hands and feet were naked pure and white, and he stood between the floors of the room, clothed with <in> purity inexpressible, he said unto me I am a messenger sent from God, be faithful and keep his commandments in all things, he told me of a sacred record which was written on plates of gold, I saw in the vision the place where they were deposited, he said the Indians were the literal descendants of Abraham he explained many things of the prophesies to

PLATE 9. *Joseph Smith, 1835–1836 Journal*, page 24.

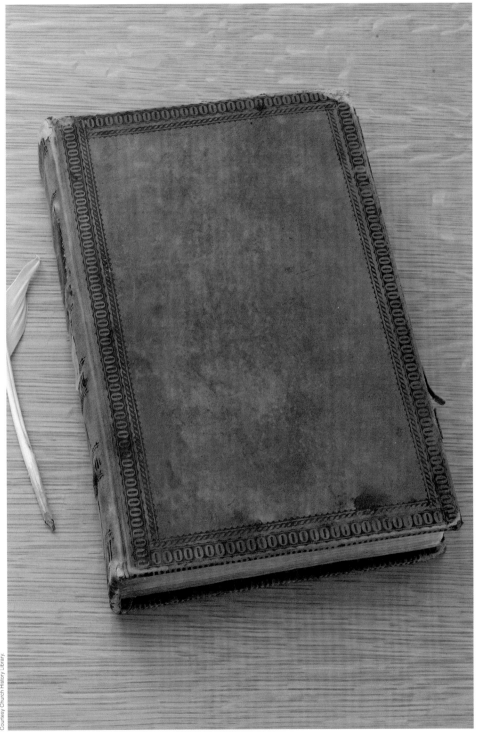

PLATE 10. *Joseph Smith, History, volume A-1, cover. Photograph by Welden C. Andersen.*

Owing to the many reports which have been put in circulation by evil disposed and designing persons in relation to the rise and progress of the Church of ^Jesus Christ of^ Latter day Saints, all of which have been designed by the authors thereof to militate against its character as a Church, and its progress in the world— I have been induced to write this history so as to disabuse the publick mind, and put all enquirers after truth into possession of the facts as they have transpired in relation both to myself and the Church, as far as I have such facts in possession. In this history I will present the various events in relation to this Church in truth and righteousness as they have transpired, or as they at present exist, being now the ^8^th year since the organization of said Church. I was born in the year of our Lord One thousand Eight hundred and five, on the twenty third day of December, in the town of Sharon, Windsor County, State of Vermont. My father Joseph Smith Senior ^(see note E, page 2. addenda ally dept)^ left the State of Vermont and moved to Palmyra, Ontario (now Wayne) County, in the State of New York when I was in my tenth year. In about four years after, my fathers arrival at Palmyra, he moved with his family into Manchester in the same County of Ontario. His family consisting of eleven souls, namely, My Father Joseph Smith, My Mother Lucy Smith whose name previous to her marriage was, Mack, daughter of Solomon Mack, My brothers Alvin (who ~~died 19th 1823 in the 25 year of his age~~) Hyrum, Myself, Samuel Harrison, William, Don Carlos, and my Sisters Sophronia, Catherine and Lucy. Sometime in the second year after our removal to Manchester, there was in the place where we lived an unusual excitement on the subject of religion. It commenced with the Methodists, but soon became general among all the sects in that region of country, indeed the whole district of Country seemed affected by it and great

PLATE 11. *Joseph Smith, History*, volume A-1, page 1.

ministers united themselves to the different religious parties, which created no small stir and division among the people, Some crying, "Lo here" and some Lo there. Some were contending for the Methodist faith, Some for the Presbyterian, and some for the Baptist; for notwithstanding the great love which the Converts to these different faiths expressed at the time of their conversion, and the great zeal manifested by the respective Clergy who were active in getting up and promoting this extraordinary scene of religious feeling in order to have every body converted as they were pleased to call it, let them join what sect they pleased; Yet when the Converts began to file off some to one party and some to another, It was seen that the seemingly good feelings of both the Priests and the Converts were more pretended then real, for a scene of great confusion and bad feeling ensued; Priest contending against priest, and convert against convert so that all their good feelings one for another (if they ever had any) were entirely lost in a strife of words and a contest about opinions.

I was at this time in my fifteenth year. My Fathers family were proselyted to the Presbyterian faith and four of them joined that Church, Namely, My Mother Lucy, My Brothers Hyrum, Samuel Harrison, and my Sister Sophronia.

During this time of great excitement my mind was called up to serious reflection and great uneasiness, but though my feelings were deep and often pungent, still I kept myself aloof from all these parties though I attended their several meetings as occasion would permit. But in process of time my mind became somewhat partial to the Methodist sect, and I felt some desire to be united with them, but so great was the confusion and strife amongst the different denominations that it was impossible for a person young as I was and so unacquainted with men and things to come to any certain conclusion who was right and who was wrong. My mind at different times was greatly excited, the cry and tumult were so great and incessant. The Presbyterians were most decided against the Baptists and Methodists, and used all their powers of either reason or sophistry to prove their errors, or at least to make the people think they were in error. On the other hand the Baptists and Methodists in their turn were equally zealous in endeavoring to establish their own tenets and disprove all others.

In the midst of this war of words, and tumult of opinions, I often said to myself, what is to be done? Who of all these parties are right? or are they all wrong together? and if any one of them be right which is it? And how shall I know it?

While I was laboring under the extreme difficulties caused by the contests of these parties of religionists, I was one day reading the Epistle of James, First Chapter and fifth verse which reads, "If any of you lack wisdom, let him ask of God, that giveth to all men liberally and upbraideth not, and it shall be given him." Never did any passage of scripture come with more power to the heart of man than this did at this time to mine. It seemed to enter with great force into every feeling of my heart. I reflected on it again and again, knowing that if any person needed wisdom from God, I did, for how to act I did not know, and unless I could get more wisdom than I then had, I would never know, for the teachers of religion of the different sects understood the same passage of Scripture so differently as to destroy all confidence in settling the question by an appeal to the Bible. At length I came to the conclusion that I must either remain in darkness and confusion or else I must do as James directs, that is, Ask of God. I at last came to the determination to ask of God, concluding that if he gave wisdom to them that lacked wisdom, and would give liberally and not upbraid, I might venture. So in accordance with this my determination to ask of God, I retired to the woods to make the attempt. It was on the morning of a beautiful clear day early in the spring of Eighteen hundred and twenty. It was the first time in my life that I had made such an attempt, for amidst all my anxieties I had never as yet made the attempt to pray vocally.

After I had retired into the place where I had previously designed to go, having looked around me and finding myself alone, I kneeled down and began to offer up the desires of my heart to God. I had scarcely done so, when immediately I was seized upon by some power which entirely overcame me and had such astonishing influence over me as to bind my tongue so that I could not speak. Thick darkness gathered around me and it seemed to me for a time as if I were doomed to sudden destruction. But exerting all my powers to call upon God to deliver me out of the power of this enemy which had seized upon me, and at the very moment when I was ready to sink into despair and abandon myself to destruction, not to an imaginary ruin but to the power of some actual being from the unseen world who had such marvelous power as I had never before felt in any being. Just at this moment of great alarm I saw a pillar of light exactly over my head above the brightness of the sun, which descended gradually untill it fell upon me. It no sooner appeared than I found myself delivered from the enemy which held me bound. When the light rested upon me I saw two personages (whose brightness and glory defy all description) standing above me in the air. One of them spake unto me calling me by name and said (pointing to the other) "This is my beloved Son, Hear him". My object in going to enquire of the Lord was to know which of all the sects was right, that I might know which to join. No sooner therefore did I get possession of myself so as to be able to speak, than I asked the personages who stood above me in the light, which of all the sects was right (for at this time it had never entered into my heart that all were wrong) and which I should join. I was answered that I must join none of them, for they were all wrong, and the Personage who addressed me said that all their Creeds were an abomination in his sight, that those professors were all corrupt, that "they draw near to me with their lips but their hearts are far from me, They teach for doctrines the commandments of men, having a form of Godliness but they deny the power thereof". He again forbade me to join with any of them, and many other things did he say unto me which I cannot write at this time. When I came to myself again I found myself lying on my back looking up into Heaven. Some few days after I had this vision I happened to be in company with one of the Methodist Preachers who was very active in the before-mentioned religious excitement and conversing with him on the subject of religion I took occasion to give him an account of the vision which I had had. I was greatly surprised at his behaviour, he treated my communication not only lightly, but with great contempt, saying it was all of the Devil, that there were no such thing as visions or revelations in these days, that all such things had ceased

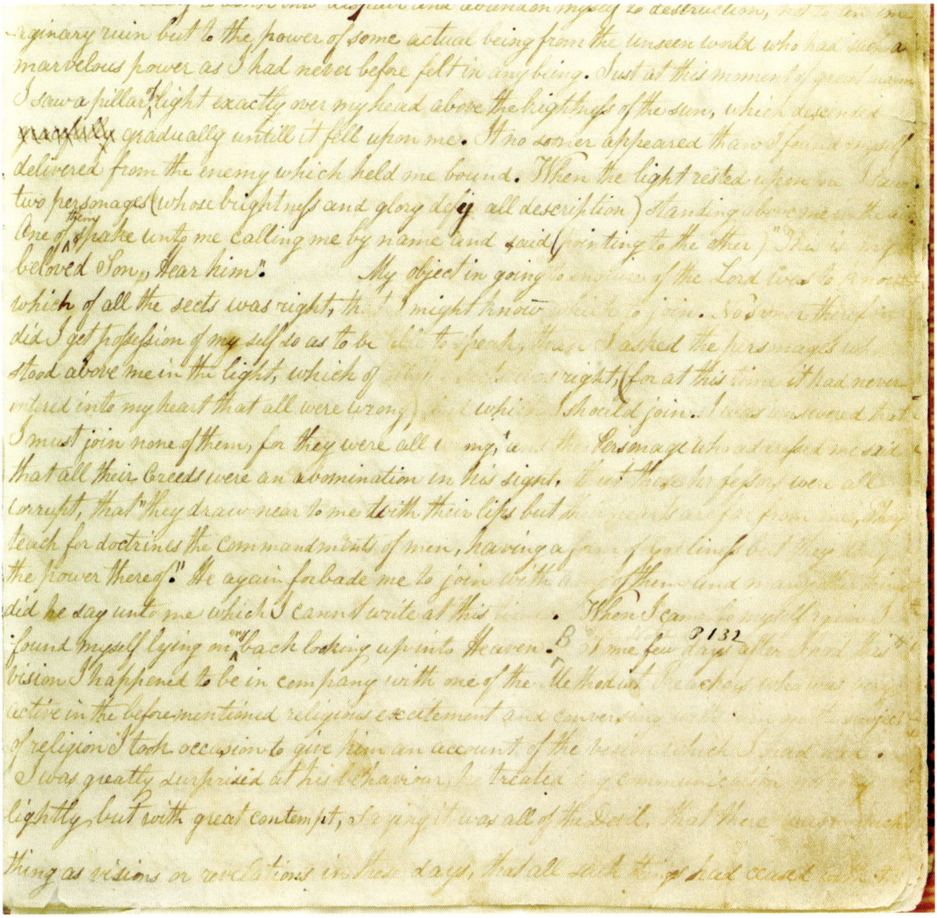

PLATE 14. Joseph Smith, History, volume A-1, page 3; note insertion.

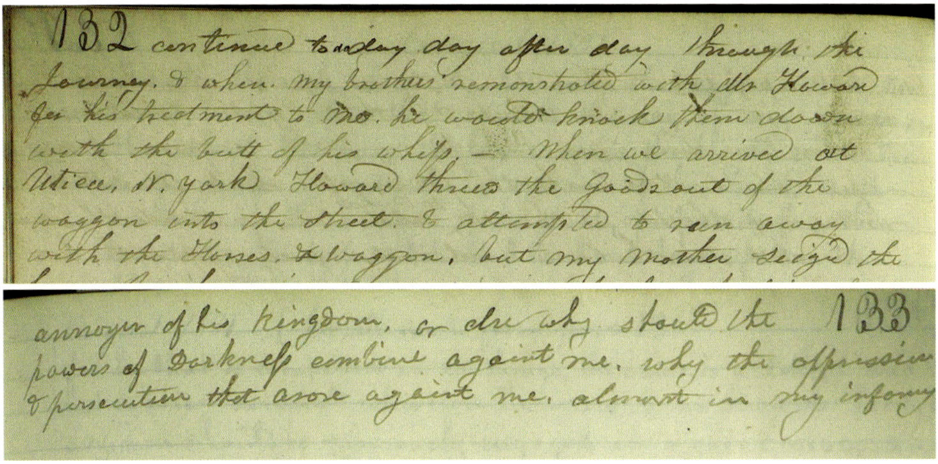

PLATE 15. Joseph Smith, History, volume A-1, pages 132–33; note insertion (1842) for page 3.

Apostles and that there never would be any more of them. I soon found however that my telling the story had excited a great deal of prejudice against me among professors of religion and was the cause of great persecution which continued to increase and though I was an obscure boy only between fourteen and fifteen years of age and my circumstances in life such as to make a boy of no consequence in the world, yet men of high standing would take notice sufficient to excite the public mind against me and create a hot persecution, and this was common among all the sects; all united to persecute me. It has often caused me to serious reflection both then and since, how very strange it was that an obscure boy of a little over fourteen years of age and one too who was doomed to the necessity of obtaining a scanty maintainance by his daily labor should be thought a character of sufficient importance to attract the attention of the great ones of the most popular sects of the day so as to create in them a spirit of the bitterest persecution and reviling. But strange or not, so it was, and was often cause of great sorrow to myself. However it was nevertheless a fact, that I had had a vision. I have thought since that I felt much like Paul when he made his defence before King Agrippa and related the account of the vision he had when he saw a light and heard a voice, but still there were but few who believed him, some said he was dishonest, others said he was mad, and he was ridiculed and reviled. But all this did not destroy the reality of his vision. He had seen a vision he knew he had, and all the persecution under Heaven could not make it otherwise, and though they should persecute him unto death yet he knew and would know to his latest breath that he had both seen a light and heard a voice speaking unto him and all the world could not make him think or believe otherwise. So it was with me, I had actualy seen a light and in the midst of that light I saw two personages, and they did in reality speak to me, or one of them did, And though I was hated and persecuted for saying that I had seen a vision, yet it was true and while they were persecuting me reviling me and speaking all manner of evil against me falsely for so saying, I was led to say in my heart, why persecute me for telling the truth? I have actually seen a vision, and who am I that I can withstand God, or why does the world think to make me deny what I have actually seen, for I had seen a vision, I knew it, and I knew that God knew it, and I could not deny it, neither dare I do it, at least I knew that by so doing would offend God and come under condemnation. I had now got my mind satisfied so far as the sectarian world was concerned, that it was not my duty to join with any of them, but continue as I was untill further directed, for I had found the testimony of James to be true, that a man who lacked wisdom might ask of God, and obtain and not be upbraided. I continued to pursue my common avocations in life untill the twenty first of September, one thousand eight hundred and twenty three, all the time suffering severe persecution at the hands of all classes of men, both religious and irreligious because I continued to affirm that I had seen a vision. During the space of time which intervened between the time I had the vision and the year Eighteen hundred and twenty three, (having been forbidden to join any of the religious sects of the day, and being of very tender years, and persecuted by those who ought to have been my friends, and to have treated me kindly

& at Br Holmers — supped &
stopped — Pres. J. Smith bore
testimony to the same — saying
that when he was a youth he
began to think about these
things but could not find out
which of all the sects were
right — he went into the grove
& enquired of the Lord which
of all the sects were right
he received for answer that
none of them were right,
that they were all wrong, &
that the Everlasting covenant
was broken — for said he understood
the fulness of the Gospel
from beginning to end — & could
Teach it & also the order of
the priesthood in all its ram
ifications — Earth & hell had apposed
him & tryed to destroy him — but
they had not done it — & they

PLATE 17. Levi Richards, Journal, entry for 11 June 1843.

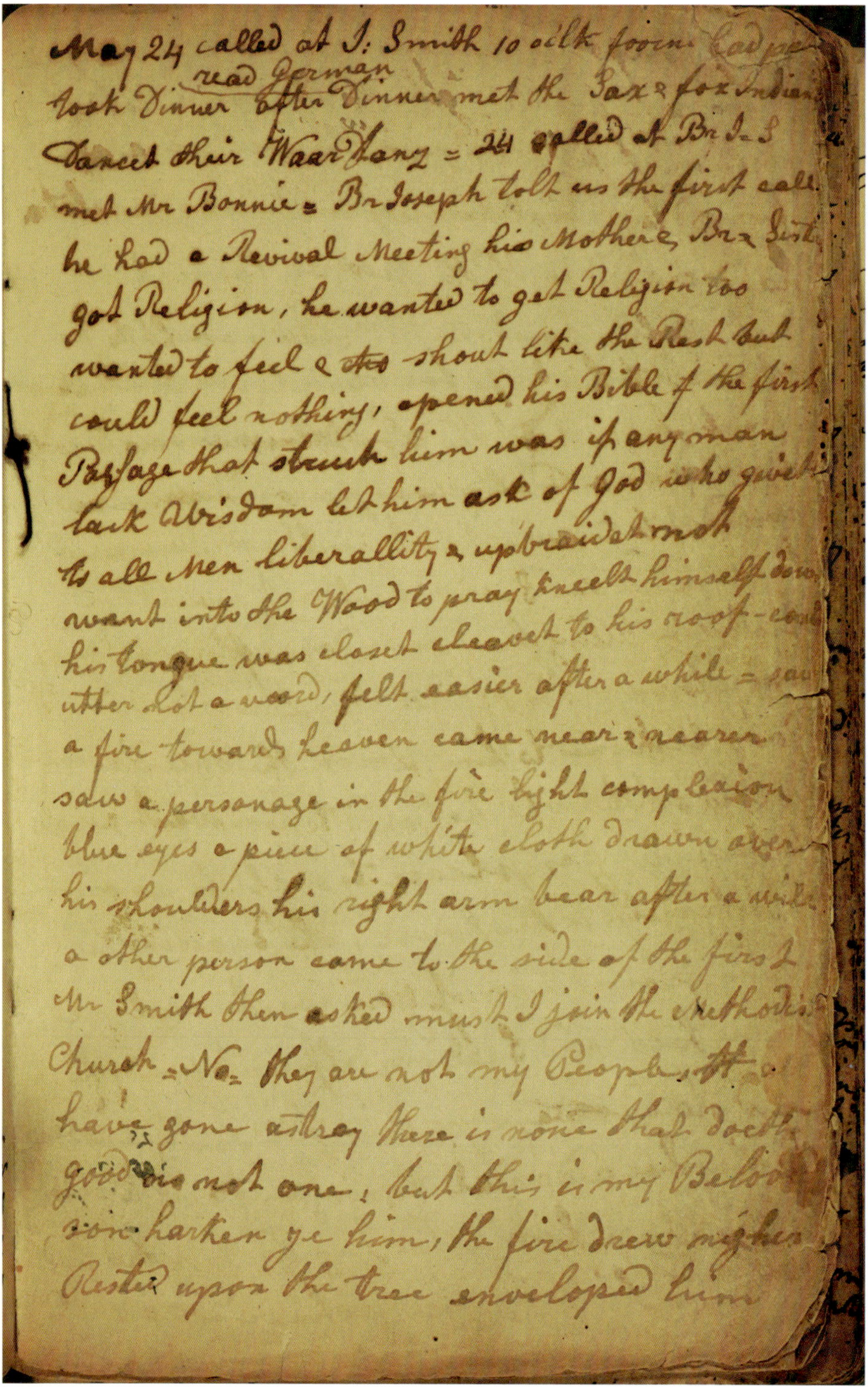
May 24 called at J: Smith 10 o'clk foun Lad pe
took Dinner read German after Dinner met the Sax & fox Indians
danced their War Danz = 24 called at Br J. S.
met Mr Bonnie = Br Joseph tolt us the first call
he had a Revival Meeting his Mother & Br & Sist
got Religion, he wanted to get Religion too
wanted to feel & to shout like the Rest but
could feel nothing, opened his Bible of the first
Passage that struck him was if any man
lack Wisdom let him ask of God who giveth
to all Men liberallity & upbraidet not
went into the Wood to pray kneelt himself down
his tongue was closet cleavet to his roof—could
utter not a word, felt easier after a while = saw
a fire towards heaven came near & nearer
saw a personage in the fire light complexion
blue eyes a piece of white cloth drawn over
his shoulders his right arm bear after a wile
a other person came to the side of the first
Mr Smith then asked must I join the Methodist
Church = No = they are not my People, all
have gone astray there is none that doeth
good no not one, but this is my Beloved
son harken ye him, the fire drew nigher
Rested upon the tree enveloped him

Courtesy Church History Library.

PLATE 18. *Alexander Neibaur, Journal, entry for 24 May 1844.*

Father Joseph Smith Siegnior moved to Palmyra Ontario [now Wayne] County in the State of New York and being an indigent circumstances were obliged to labour hard for the support of a large Family having nine chilldren and as it required the exertions of all that were able to render any assistance for the support of the Family therefore we were deprived of the bennifit of an education suffice it to say I was mearly instructtid in reading ~~and~~ writing and the ground <rules> of Arithmatic which constuted my whole literary acquirements. At about the age of twelve years my mind became seriously imprest [p. 1] with regard to the all importent concerns for the wellfare of my immortal Soul which led me to searching the scriptures believeing as I was taught, that they contained the word of God thus applying myself to them and my intimate acquaintance with those of different denominations led me to marvel excedingly for I discovered that <they did not ~~adorn~~ > ~~instead~~ of adorning their profession by a holy walk and Godly conversation agreeable to what I found contained in that sacred depository this was a grief to my Soul thus from the age of twelve years to fifteen I pondered many things in my heart concerning the sittuation of the world of mankind the contentions and divi[si]ons the wicke[d]ness and abominations and the darkness which pervaded the ~~of the~~ minds of mankind my mind become excedingly distressed for I become convicted of my sins and by searching the scriptures I found that ~~mand~~ <mankind> did not come unto the Lord but that they had apostatised from the true and liveing faith and there was no society or denomination that built upon the gospel of

Jesus Christ as recorded in the new testament and I felt to mourn for my own sins and for the sins of the world for I learned in the scriptuers that God was the same yesterday to day and forever that he was no respecter to persons for he was God for I looked upon the sun the glorious luminary of the earth and also the moon rolling in their magesty through the heavens and also the stars shining in their courses and the earth also upon which I stood and the beast of the field and the fowls of heaven and the fish of the waters and also man walking forth upon the face of the earth in magesty and in the strength of beauty whose power and intiligence in governing the things which are so exceding great and [p.2] marvilous even in the likeness of him who created ~~him~~ <them> and when I considered upon these things my heart exclaimed well hath the wise man said ~~the~~ <it is a> fool <that> saith in his hear there is no God my heart exlaimed all all these bear testimony and bespeak an omnipotant and omnipreasant power a being who makith Laws and decreeth and bindeth all things in their bounds who filleth Eternity who was and is and will be from all Eternity to Eternity and when I, considered all these things and that <that> being seeketh such to worship him as worship him in spirit and in truth therefore I cried unto the Lord for mercy for there was none else to whom I could go and to obtain mercy and the Lord heard my cry in the wilderness and while in <the> attitude of calling upon the Lord <in the 16th year of my age> a piller of ~~fire~~ light above the brightness of the sun at noon day come down from above and rested upon me and I was filled with the spirit of god and the <Lord> opened the heavens upon me and I saw the Lord and he spake unto me saying Joseph <my son> thy sins are forgiven thee. go thy <way> walk in my statutes and keep my commandments behold I am the Lord of glory I was crucifyed for the world that all those who believe on my name may have Eternal life <behold> the world lieth in sin and at this time and none doeth good no not one they have turned asside from the gospel and keep not <my> commandments they draw near to me with their lips while their hearts are far from me and mine anger is kindling against the inhabitants of the earth to visit them according to th[e]ir ungodliness and to bring to pass that which <hath> been spoken by the mouth of the prophets and Ap[o]stles behold and lo I come quickly as it [is] written of me in the cloud <clothed> in the glory of my Father and my soul was filled with love and for many days I could rejoice with great Joy and the Lord was with me but [I] could find none that would believe the hevnly vision nevertheless I pondered these things in my heart.

## 1835 Accounts

Three years later, in 1835, an eccentric visitor from the east inquired of Joseph about his vision. His scribe captured some of Joseph's response in his journal entry for November 9. In this account Joseph cast the vision as the first in a series of events that led to the translation of the Book of Mormon. He emphasized the opposition he felt in the grove and how he attempted to pray but could not at first. This account tells that one divine personage appeared in a pillar of fire, followed shortly by another, and that Joseph envisioned many angels as well. Joseph added as an afterthought that he was about fourteen at the time of his vision. A week later, on November 14, Joseph told another inquirer of the vision, though his scribe recorded only that Joseph gave the fellow, Erastus Holmes, an account of his "first visitation of Angels," rather than describing the vision itself.

Both 1835 accounts were also incorporated into a draft of Joseph's history. Even so, they remained generally unknown to Latter-day Saints until LDS historians published them in the late 1960s.[8] See Plates 7–9.

## Transcription of 9 November 1835 Account

I commenced giving him a relation of the circumstances connected with the coming forth of the book of Mormon, as follows—being wrought up in my mind, respecting the subject of religion and looking at the different systems taught the children of men, I knew not who was right or who was wrong and I considered it of the first importance that I should be right, in matters that involve eternal consequ[e]nces; being thus perplexed in mind I retired to the silent grove and bow[e]d down before the Lord, under a realising sense that he had said (if the bible be true) ask and you shall receive knock and it shall be opened seek and you shall find and again, if any man lack wisdom let him ask of God who giveth to all men libarally and

---

8. Dean C. Jessee, "The Early Accounts of Joseph Smith's First Vision," *BYU Studies* 9, no. 3 (1969): 275–94; James B. Allen, "The Significance of Joseph Smith's 'First Vision' in Mormon Thought," *Dialogue: A Journal of Mormon Thought* 1 (Autumn 1966): 40–41.

upbradeth not; information was what I most desired at this time, and with a fixed determination to obtain it, I called upon the Lord for the first time, in the place above stated or in other words I made a fruitless attempt to p[r]ay, my toung seemed to be swolen in my mouth, so that I could not utter, I heard a noise behind me like some person walking towrds me, I strove again to pray, but could not, the noise of walking seemed to draw nearer, I sprung up on my feet, ~~and~~ [p.23] and looked around, but saw no person or thing that was calculated to produce the noise of walking, I kneeled again my mouth was opened and my toung liberated, and I called on the Lord in mighty prayer, a pillar of fire appeared above my head, it presently rested down up me ~~head~~, and filled me with Joy unspeakable, a personage appeard in the midst of this pillar of flame which was spread all around, and yet nothing consumed, another personage soon appeard like unto the first, he said unto me thy sins are forgiven thee, he testifyed unto me that Jesus Christ is the Son of God; <and I saw many angels in this vision> I was about 14 years old when I received this first communication.

## Transcription of 14 November 1835 account

I commenced and gave him a brief relation of my experience while in my [p. 36] juvenile years, say from 6 years old up to the time I received the first visitation of Angels which was when I was about 14. years old and also the visitations that I received afterward, concerning the book of Mormon, and a short account of the rise and progress of the church.

## 1838 Account

Joseph Smith published two accounts of the vision during his lifetime. The first of these to be written and the best known is in Joseph's history. Scribe George Robinson noted that he and Joseph and Sidney Rigdon spent 27 April 1838 "writing a history of this Church from the earliest period of its existence."[9] Dean C. Jessee wrote that by May 2 "the writing had progressed to the eighth page of the manuscript," including the account of the first vision.[10] James Mulholland copied this text into Manuscript History Book A1 sometime before his death late in 1839. Howard Coray edited this account about 1841. Joseph published the early part of this history in the *Times and Seasons* on 15 March 1842. Willard Richards edited this account later that year when he began service as Joseph's secretary, which is why the version now excerpted and canonized in the Pearl of Great Price varies from the version in the *Times and Seasons*. Much more than the others, this account emphasizes unusual religious excitement external to Joseph as a catalyst for the vision. The other accounts suggest a more internal process. Of course, the external and internal forces are not mutually exclusive. This account also emphasizes Joseph's quest for a true church, whereas the others emphasize a quest for redemption. Again, these seem like compatible quests. This account is rich with evidence of both factual memory (what

---

9. Jessee, Ashurst-McGee, Jensen, *Journals*, 1:260–61; spelling standardized.
10. Joseph Smith, *Personal Writings of Joseph Smith*, ed. Dean C. Jessee, 2d ed. (Salt Lake City: Deseret Book, 2002), 226.

Joseph experienced at the time) and interpretive memory (what the experience meant to Joseph over time). See Plates 10–16.

## Transcription of 1838 Account

Owing to the many reports which have been put in circulation by evil disposed and designing persons in relation to the rise and progress of the Church of <Jesus Christ of> Latter day Saints, all of which have been designed by the authors thereof to militate against its character as a church, and its progress in the world; I have been induced to write this history so as to disabuse the publick mind, and put all enquirers after truth into possession of the facts as they have transpired in relation both to myself and the Church as far as I have such facts in possession.

In this history I will present the various events in relation to this Church in truth and righteousness as they have transpired, or as they at present exist, being now the eighth year since the organization of said Church. I was born in the year of our Lord One thousand Eight hundred and five, on the twenty third day of December, in the town of Sharon, Windsor County, State of Vermont. <see page Note A 131> My father Joseph Smith Senior left the State of Vermont and move to Palmyra, Ontario, (now Wayne) County, in the State of New York when I was in my tenth year. <or thereabout.>

In about four years after my father's arrival at Palmyra, he moved with his family into Manchester in the same County of Ontario. His family consisting of eleven souls, namely, My Father Joseph Smith, My Mother Lucy Smith whose name previous to her marriage was Mack, daughter of Solomon Mack, My brothers Alvin (who <died Nov. 19th: 1823 in the 25 year of his age.> ~~is now dead~~ ) Hyrum, Myself, Samuel—Harrison, William, Don Carloss, and my Sisters Soph[r]onia, Cathrine and Lucy. Sometime in the second year after our removal to Manchester, there was in the place where we lived an unusual excitement on the subject of religion. It commenced with the Methodists, but soon became general among all the sects in that region of ~~the~~ country, indeed the whole district of Country seemed affected by it and great [p. 1] multitudes united themselves to the different religious parties, which created no small stir and division among the people, Some crying, "Lo here" and some Lo there. Some were contending for the Methodist faith, Some for the Presbyterian, and some for the Baptist; for notwithstanding the great love which the converts to these different faiths expressed at the time of their conversion, and the great Zeal manifested by the respective Clergy who were active in getting up and promoting this extraordinary scene of religious feeling in order to have everybody converted as they were pleased to call it, let them join what sect they pleased yet when the Converts began to file off some to one party and some to another, it was seen that the seemingly good feelings of both the Priests and the Converts were ~~more pretence~~ more pretended than real, for a scene of great confusion and bad feeling ensued; Priest contending against priest, and convert against convert so that all their good feelings one for another (if they ever had any) were entirely lost in a strife of words and a contest about opinions.

I was at this time in my fifteenth year. My Fathers family ~~was~~ <ere> proselyted to the Presbyterian faith and four of them joined that Church, Namely, My

Mother Lucy, My Brothers Hyrum, Samuel Harrison, and my Sister Sop[r]onia.

During this time of great excitement my mind was called up to serious reflection and great uneasiness, but though my feelings were deep and often pungent, still I kept myself aloof from all these parties although I attended their several meetings <as often> as occasion would permit. But in process of time my mind became somewhat partial to the Methodist sect, and I felt some desire to be united with them, but so great was the confusion and strife amongst the different denominations that it was impossible for a person young as I was and so unacquainted with men and things to come to any certain conclusion who was right and who was wrong. My mind at different times was greatly excited for the cry and tumult were so great and incessant. The Presbyterians were most decided against the Baptists and Methodists, and used all their powers of either reason or sophistry to prove their errors, or at least to make the people think they were in error. On the other hand the Baptists and Methodists in their turn were equally Zealous in endeavoring to establish their own tenets and disprove all others.

In the midst of this war of words, and tumult of opinions, I often said to myself, what is to be done? Who of all these parties are right? Or are they all wrong together? And if any one of them be right which is it? And how shall I know it?

While I was laboring under the extreme difficulties caused by the contests of these parties of religionists, I was one day reading the Epistle of James, First Chapter and fifth verse which reads, "If any of you lack wisdom, let him ask of God, that giveth to all men liberally and upbraideth not, and it shall be given him."

Never did any passage of scripture come with more power to the heart of man [than] this did at this time to mine. It seemed to enter with great force into every feeling of my heart. I reflected on it again and again, knowing that if any person needed wisdom from God, I did, for how to act I did not know and unless I could get more wisdom than I then had would never know, for the teachers of religion of the different sects understood the same [end p. 2] passage of Scripture so differently as <to> destroy all confidence in settling the question by an appeal to the Bible. At length I came to the Conclusion that I must either remain in darkness and confusion or else I must do as James directs, that is, Ask of God. I at last came to the determination to ask of God, concluding that if he gave wisdom to them that lacked wisdom, and would give liberally and not upbraid, I might venture. So, in accordance with this, my determination to ask of God, I retired to the woods to make the attempt. It was on the morning of a beautiful clear day early in the spring of Eightteen hundred and twenty. It was the first time in my life that I had <made> such an attempt, for amidst all <my> anxieties I had never as yet made the attempt to pray vocally.

After I had retired into the place where I had previously designed to go, having looked around me and finding myself alone, I kneeled down and began to offer up the desires of my heart to God, I had scarcely done so, when immediately I was <siezed> upon by some power which entirely overcame me and <had> such astonishing influence over me as to bind my tongue so that I could not speak. Thick darkness gathered around me and it seemed to me for a time as if I were doomed to sudden destruction. But exerting all my powers to call upon God to deliver me out of the power of this enemy which had siezed upon me, and at the very moment when I was ready to sink into despair and abandon myself to destruction, not to an imaginary ruin but to the power of some actual being from the unseen world who had such a marvelous power as I had never before felt in any being. Just at this moment of great alarm I saw a pillar <of> light exactly over my head above the brightness of the sun, which descended ~~gracefully~~ gradually untill it fell upon me. It no sooner appeared than I found myself delivered from the enemy which held me bound. When the light rested upon me I saw two personages (whose brightness and glory defy all description) standing above me in the air. One of <them> spake unto me calling me by name and said (pointing to the other) "This is my beloved Son, Hear him." My object in going to enquire of the Lord was to know which of all the sects was right, that I might know which to join. No sooner therefore did I get possession of myself so as to be able to speak, than I asked the personages who stood above me in the light, which of all the sects was right, (for at this time it had never entered into my heart that all were wrong) and which I should join. I was answered that I must join none of them, for they were all wrong, and the Personage who addressed me said that all their Creeds were an abomination in his sight, that those professors were all Corrupt, that "they draw near to me with their lips but their hearts are far from me, They teach for doctrines the commandments of men, having a form of Godliness but they deny the power thereof." He again forbade me to join with any of them and many other things did he say unto me which I cannot write at this time. When I came to myself again I found myself lying on <my> back looking up into Heaven.

[footnote added in 1842] When the light had departed I had no strength, but soon recovering in some degree. I went home.—& as I leaned up to the fire piece Mother Enquired what the matter was. I replied never mind all is well.—I am well enough off. I then told my mother I have learned for myself that Presbyterianism is not true.—It seems as though the adversary was aware at a very early period of my life that I was destined to prove a disturber & [p. 132] annoyer of his kingdom, or else why should the powers of Darkness combine against me, why the oppression & persecution that arose against me, almost in my infancy?}>

Some few days after I had this vision I happened to be in company with one of the Methodist Preachers who was very active in the before mentioned religious excitement and conversing with him on the subject of religion I took occasion to give him an account of the vision which I had had. I was greatly surprised at his behaviour, he treated my communication not only lightly but with great contempt, saying it was all of the Devil, that there was no such thing as visions or revelations in these days, that all such things had ceased with the [end p. 3] apostles and that there never would be any more of them. I soon found however that my telling the story had excited a great deal of prejudice against me among professors of religion and was the cause of great persecution which continued to increase and though I was an obscure boy only between fourteen and fifteen years of age <or thereabouts,> and my circumstances in life such as to make a boy of no consequence in the world, yet men of high standing would take notice sufficiently to excite the public mind against me and create a hot persecution, and this was common <among> all the sects: all united to persecute me. It has often caused me ~~m~~ serious reflection both then and since, how very strange it was that an obscure boy of a little over fourteen years of age and one too who was doomed to the necessity of obtaining a scanty maintenance by his daily labor should be thought a character of sufficient importance to attract the attention of the great ones of the most popular sects of the day so as to create in them a spirit of the bitterest persecution and reviling. But strange or not, so it was, and was often cause of great sorrow to myself. However it was nevertheless a fact, that I had had a vision. I have thought since that I felt much like Paul ~~did~~ when he made his defence before King Aggrippa and related the account of the vision he had when he saw a light and heard a voice, but still there were but few who believed him, some said he was dishonest, others said he was mad, and he was ridiculed and reviled, But all this did not destroy the reality of his vision. He had seen a vision and he knew he had, and <all> the persecution under Heaven could not make it otherwise, and though they should persecute him unto death yet he knew and would know to his latest breath that he had both seen a light and heard a voice speaking unto him and all the world could not make him think or believe otherwise. So it was with me, I had actualy seen a light and in the midst of that light I saw two personages, and they did in reality speak <un> to me, or one of them did, And though I was hated and persecuted for saying that I had seen a vision, yet it was true and while they were persecuting me reviling me and speaking all manner of evil against me falsely for so saying, I was led to say in my heart, why persecute <me> for telling the truth? I have actually seen a vision, "and who am I that I can withstand God" or why does the world think to make me deny what I have actually seen, for I had seen a vision, I knew it, and I knew that God knew it, and I could not deny it, neither dare I do it, at least I knew that by so doing <I> would offend God and come under condemnation. I had now got my mind satisfied so far as the sectarian world was concerned, that it was not my duty to join with any of them, but continue as I was untill further directed, ~~for~~ I had found the testimony of James to be true.

## 1842 Account

Joseph responded to *Chicago Democrat* editor John Wentworth's request for a "sketch of the rise, progress, persecution and faith of the Latter-day Saints" as source material for a friend, George Barstow, who was writing a history of New Hampshire.[11] Many of Wentworth's papers seem to have been destroyed in the 1871 Chicago fire, and there is no known evidence that Barstow used Joseph's account, but Joseph had it printed in the 1 March 1842 issue of the *Times and Seasons* newspaper, making it the first account published in the United States. In July 1843 a historian named Israel Daniel Rupp wrote to Joseph, asking for a chapter on the history of Mormonism for inclusion in his book, *He Pasa Ekklesia: An Original History of the Religious Denominations at Present Existing in the United States.* Joseph responded to Rupp's refreshing invitation to tell his own story by supplying Rupp with essentially the same

---

11. John W. Welch, ed., *Opening the Heavens: Accounts of Divine Manifestations, 1820–1844* (Provo, Utah: Brigham Young University Press, 2005), 17.

account in the Wentworth letter, which Rupp subsequently included in his book.[12]

This account is brief but telling. It says that the two divine beings Joseph envisioned looked exactly alike and that they told him that the existing churches believed in incorrect doctrines.

## Transcription of 1842 Account

I was born in the town of Sharon Windsor co., Vermont, on the 23d of December, A.D. 1805. When ten years old my parents removed to Palmyra New York, where we resided about four years, and from thence we removed to the town of Manchester.

My father was a farmer and taught me the art of husbandry. When about fourteen years of age I began to reflect upon the importance of being prepared for a future state, and upon enquiring the plan of salvation I found that there was a great clash in religious sentiment; if I went to one society they referred me to one plan, and another to another; each one pointing to his own particular creed as the summum bonum of perfection: considering that all could not be right, and that God could not be the author of so much confusion I determined to investigate the subject more fully, believing that if God had a church it would not be split up into factions, and that if he taught one society to

---

12. Joseph Smith, "Latter Day Saints," in I. Daniel Rupp, comp., *He Pasa Ekklesia: An Original History of the Religious Denominations at Present Existing in the United States* (Philadelphia: J. Y. Humphreys, 1844), 404–10; Jessee, *Papers of Joseph Smith*, 1:448–49; Karen Lynn Davidson, David J. Whittaker, Mark Ashurst-McGee, and Richard L. Jensen, eds., *Histories, 1832–1844*, vol. 1 of the Histories series of *The Joseph Smith Papers*, edited by Dean C. Jessee, Ronald K. Esplin, and Richard Lyman Bushman (Salt Lake City: Church Historian's Press, 2012), 490.

worship one way, and administer in one set of ordinances, he would not teach another principles which were diametrically opposed. Believing the word of God I had confidence in the declaration of James; "If any man lack wisdom let him ask of God who giveth to all men liberally and upbraideth not and it shall be given him," I retired to a secret place in a grove and began to call upon the Lord, while fervently engaged in supplication my mind was taken away from the objects with which I was surrounded, and I was enwrapped in a [p. 706] heavenly vision and saw two glorious personages who exactly resembled each other in features, and likeness, surrounded with a brilliant light which eclipsed the sun at noon-day. They told me that all religious denominations were believing in incorrect doctrines, and that none of them was acknowledged of God as his church and kingdom. And I was expressly commanded to "go not after them," at the same time receiving a promise that the fulness of the gospel should at some future time be made known unto me.

### Contemporary Secondary Accounts

Besides the accounts that come directly from Joseph, there are several known contemporary secondary accounts, meaning they were written during Joseph's lifetime by people who heard him describe his vision.[13]

---

13. The historical record includes other accounts, published long after Joseph's death, by people who said they heard Joseph tell of the vision or heard the stories of others who did. These include Mary Isabella Hales Horne's recollection in *Woman's Exponent* 39 (June 1910): 6; Joseph Curtis, Reminiscences and Journal, MS, 5, Church History Library; Edward Stevenson, "The Life and History of Elder Edward Stevenson," MS, 21, Church History Library. See also Edward Stevenson, *Reminiscences of Joseph the Prophet and the Coming Forth of the Book of Mormon* (Salt Lake City: By the author,

A WELL-DOCUMENTED THEOPHANY

## Orson Pratt, 1840

As an apostle-missionary in Scotland, Orson Pratt wrote and published in September 1840 *A[n] Interesting Account of Several Remarkable Visions*. It recounts Joseph Smith's first vision by echoing passages from Joseph's earlier accounts and prefiguring passages in later ones, as well as by including some unique details. Orson Pratt must have had access to Joseph's accounts, either in person or through the documents of the pre-1840 versions (or both), and possibly to an unknown source of material for the 1842 Wentworth letter. Alternatively, Orson's own rendering of the vision may have shaped the account in the Wentworth letter. The two accounts clearly share phrasing. Pratt's account of the vision is the most thorough of the contemporary secondary accounts.[14]

### Transcription of Orson Pratt Account

When somewhere about fourteen or fifteen years old, he [Joseph Smith] began seriously to reflect upon the necessity of being prepared for a future state of existence: but how, or in what way, to prepare himself (see JS Papers, Histories 1:522), was a question, as yet, undetermined in his own mind: he perceived that it was a question of infinite importance, and that the salvation of his soul depended upon a correct understanding of the same. He saw, that if he understood not the [p. 3]

---

1893), 4–5; Edward Stevenson, *Juvenile Instructor* 29 (15 July 1894): 444–45; *Diary of Charles Lowell Walker*, 2 February 1893, ed. A. Karl Larsen and Katharine Miles Larsen, 2 vols. (Logan, Utah: Utah State University Press, 1980), vol. 2: 755–56.

14. Orson Pratt, *A[n] Interesting Account of Several Remarkable Visions, and The Late Discovery of Ancient American Records* (Edinburgh: Ballantyne and Hughes, 1840), 3–5; Jessee, ed., *Papers of Joseph Smith*, 1:389–91.

way, it would be impossible to walk in it, except by chance; and the thought of resting his hopes of eternal life upon chance, or uncertainties, was more than he could endure. If he went to the religious denominations to seek information, each one pointed to its particular tenets, saying—"This is the way, walk ye in it;" while, at the same time, the doctrines of each were, in many respects, in direct opposition to one another. It, also, occurred to his mind, that God was not the author of but one doctrine, and therefore could not acknowledge but one denomination as his church; and that such denomination must be a people, who believe, and teach, that one doctrine, (whatever it may be,) and build upon the same. He then reflected upon the immense number of doctrines, now, in the world, which had given rise to many hundreds of different denominations. The great question to be decided in his mind, was—if any of these denominations be the Church of Christ, which one is it? Until he could become satisfied, in relation to this question, he could not rest contented. To trust to the decisions of fallible man, and build his hopes upon the same, without any certainty, and knowledge of his own, would not satisfy the anxious desires that pervaded his breast. To decide, without any positive and definite evidence, on which he could rely, upon a subject involving the future welfare of his soul, was revolting to his feelings. The only alternative, that seemed to be left him, was to read the Scriptures, and endeavour to follow their directions. He, accordingly, commenced perusing the sacred pages of the Bible, with sincerity, believing the things that he read. His mind soon caught hold of the following passage:—"If any of you lack wisdom, let him ask of God, that giveth to all men liberally, and

AN

INTERESTING ACCOUNT

OF

SEVERAL REMARKABLE VISIONS,

AND OF

**THE LATE DISCOVERY**

OF

Ancient American Records.

By O. PRATT,

MINISTER OF THE GOSPEL.

[THIRD AMERICAN EDITION.]

NEW-YORK:
JOSEPH W. HARRISON, PRINTER,
No. 465 PEARL-STREET.

1842.

*Title page, Orson Pratt's account, third American printing of An Interesting Account of Several Remarkable Visions, originally published in Scotland, 1840.*

upbraideth not; and it shall be given him."—James i. 5. From this promise he learned, that it was the privilege of all men to ask God for wisdom, with the sure and certain expectation of receiving, liberally; without being upbraided for so doing. This was cheering information to him: tidings that gave him great joy. It was like a light shining forth in a dark place, to guide him to the path in which he should walk. He, now, saw that if he inquired of God, there was, not only, a possibility, but a probability; yea, more, a certainty, that he should [p. 4] obtain a knowledge, which, of all the doctrines, was the doctrine of Christ; and, which, of all the churches, was the church of Christ. He, therefore, retired to a secret place, in a grove, but a short distance from his father's house, and knelt down, and began to call upon the Lord. At first, he was severely tempted by the powers of darkness, which endeavoured to overcome him; but he continued to seek for deliverance, until darkness gave way from his mind; and he was enabled to pray, in fervency of the spirit, and in faith. And, while thus pouring out his soul, anxiously desiring an answer from God, he, at length, saw a very bright and glorious light in the heavens above; which, at first, seemed to be at a considerable distance. He continued praying, while the light appeared to be gradually descending towards him; and, as it drew nearer, it increased in brightness, and magnitude, so that, by the time that it reached the tops of the trees, the whole wilderness, for some distance around, was illuminated in a most glorious and brilliant manner. He expected to have seen the leaves and boughs of the trees consumed, as soon as the light came in contact with them; but, perceiving that it did not produce that effect, he was encouraged with the hopes of being able to endure its presence. It continued descending, slowly, until it rested upon the earth, and he was enveloped in the midst of it. When it first came upon him, it produced a peculiar sensation throughout his whole system; and, immediately, his mind was caught away, from the natural objects with which he was surrounded; and he was enwrapped in a heavenly vision, and saw two glorious personages, who exactly resembled each other in their features or likeness. He was informed, that his sins were forgiven. He was also informed upon the subjects, which had for some time previously agitated his mind, viz.—that all the religious denominations were believing in incorrect doctrines; and, consequently, that none of them was acknowledged of God, as his church and kingdom. And he was expressly commanded, to go not after them; and he received a promise that the true doctrine—the fullness of the gospel, should, at some future time, be made known to him; after which the vision withdrew, leaving his mind in a state of calmness and peace, indescribable.

## Orson Hyde, 1842

In 1842 Orson Hyde, an apostle, was returning to the United States from the Holy Land via Germany when he published *Ein Ruf aus der Wüste* (A Cry from the Wilderness) in Frankfurt. He had undertaken a mission to the Jews of Europe and Palestine. En route, he composed the pamphlet on the history and doctrine of the Church in English, deriving his description of Joseph's first vision from Orson Pratt's.[15]

---

15. Orson Hyde, *Ein Ruf aus der Wüste, eine Stimme aus dem Schoose der Erde* (A Cry from the Wilderness, a Voice from the Dust of the Earth) (Frankfurt: n.p., 1842), 14–16.

He stopped in Germany to study the language on the way to Jerusalem and translated his booklet in Germany on the way back to the United States, making it the first account published in a language other than English.

## Transcription of Orson Hyde Account

When he had reached his fifteenth year, he began to think seriously about the importance of preparing for a future [existence]; but it was very difficult for him to decide how he should go about such an important undertaking. He recognized clearly that it would be impossible for him to walk the proper path without being acquainted with it beforehand; and to base his hopes for eternal life on chance or blind uncertainty would have been more than he had ever been inclined to do.

He discovered the world of religion working under a flood of errors which by virtue of their contradictory opinions and principles laid the foundation for the rise of such different sects and denominations whose feelings toward each other all too often were poisoned by hate, contention, resentment and anger. He felt that there was only one truth and that those who understood it correctly, all understood it in the same way. Nature had endowed him with a keen critical intellect and so he looked through the lens of reason and common sense and with pity and contempt upon those systems of religion, which were so opposed to each other and yet were all obviously based on the scriptures.

After he had sufficiently convinced himself to his

---

This text is a translation from the German by Marvin Folsom, professor emeritus of German, Brigham Young University. This text is also reprinted in Jessee, *Papers of Joseph Smith,* 1:402–25, and in Welch, *Opening the Heavens,* 22–23.

# Ein
# Ruf aus der Wüste,
### eine
## Stimme aus dem Schoose der Erde.

**Kurzer Ueberblick**
des Ursprungs und der Lehre der Kirche „Jesus Christ of Latter Day Saints" in Amerika, gekannt von Manchen unter der Benennung: »Die Mormonen.«

Von
**Orson Hyde,**
Priester dieser Kirche.

Lese, betrachte, bete und handle!

**Frankfurt, 1842.**
Im Selbstverlage des Verfassers.

*Title page, Orson Hyde's account, Ein Ruf aus der Wuste (A Cry from the Wilderness), originally published in Frankfurt, Germany 1842.*

own satisfaction that darkness covered the earth and gross darkness [covered] the nations, the hope of ever finding a sect or denomination that was in possession of unadulterated truth left him.

Consequently he began in an attitude of faith his own investigation of the word of God [feeling that it was] the best way to arrive at a knowledge of the truth. He had not proceeded very far in this laudable endeavor when his eyes fell upon the following verse of St. James [1:5]: "If any of you lack wisdom, let him ask of God, that giveth to all men liberally, and upbraideth not; and it shall be given him." He considered this scripture an authorization for him to solemnly call upon his creator to present his needs before him with the certain expectation of some success. And so he began to pour out to the Lord with fervent determination the earnest desires of his soul. On one occasion, he went to a small grove of trees near his father's home and knelt down before God in solemn prayer. The adversary then made several strenuous efforts to cool his ardent soul. He filled his mind with doubts [p. 15] and brought to mind all manner of inappropriate images to prevent him from obtaining the object of his endeavors; but the overflowing mercy of God came to buoy him up and gave new impetus to his failing strength. However, the dark cloud soon parted and light and peace filled his frightened heart. Once again he called upon the Lord with faith and fervency of spirit.

At this sacred moment, the natural world around him was excluded from his view, so that he would be open to the presentation of heavenly and spiritual things. Two glorious heavenly personages stood before him, resembling each other exactly in features and stature. They told him that his prayers had been answered and that the Lord had decided to grant him a special blessing. He was also told that he should not join any of the religious sects or denominations, because all of them erred in doctrine and none was recognized by God as his church and kingdom. He was further commanded, to wait patiently until some future time, when the true doctrine of Christ and the complete truth of the gospel would be revealed to him. The vision closed and peace and calm filled his mind.

## Lévi Richards, 1843

Levi Richards was a cousin of Brigham Young and a brother of Willard Richards, Joseph Smith's secretary and Church historian. Levi joined the Church in 1835 and relocated with the Saints from Ohio to Missouri and then to Illinois. There he worked as a physician and held prominent positions in the militia and on the Nauvoo city council. He attended a discourse by George Adams on the evening of Sunday, 11 June 1843, after which Joseph Smith described his first vision. Levi described the experience in his journal (see Plate 17).[16]

### Transcription of Levi Richards Account

At 6 P.M. heard Eld. G J Adams upon the book of Mormon proved from the 24th, 28th & 29 of Isaiah that the everlasting covenant which was set up by Christ & the apostles had been broken . . .

---

16. Levi Richards, Journal, 11 June 1843, MS, Church History Library. See also Andrew F. Ehat and Lyndon W. Cook, eds., *The Words of Joseph Smith: The Contemporary Accounts of the Nauvoo Discourses of the Prophet Joseph,* Religious Studies Monograph Series, no. 6 (Provo, Utah: Religious Studies Center, Brigham Young University, 1980), 215; Welch, ed., *Opening the Heavens,* 23–24.

—Pres. J. Smith bore testimony to the same—saying that when he was a youth he began to think about these things but could not find out which of all the sects were right—he went into the grove &, enquired of the Lord which of all the sects were right—he received for answer that none of them were right, that they were all wrong, & that the Everlasting covenant was broken

## David Nye White, 1843

In August 1843 David Nye White, editor of the *Pittsburgh Weekly Gazette,* was traveling through what was then the western United States when he interviewed Joseph Smith. White knew that his readers would be interested in what he called the "kingdom of the 'Latter-day Saints'" and their prophet's story. He published a report of his interview in the September 1843 issue of the *Gazette,* including the following version of Joseph's vision account.[17]

### Transcription of David Nye White Account

The Lord does reveal himself to me. I know it. He revealed himself first to me when I was about fourteen years old, a mere boy. I will tell you about it. There was a reformation among the different religious denominations in the neighborhood where I lived, and I became serious, and was desirous to know what Church to join. While thinking of this matter, I opened the [New] Testament promiscuously on these words, in James, "Ask of the Lord who giveth to all men liberally and

---

17. "The Prairies, Nauvoo, Joe Smith, the Temple, the Mormons, &c.," *Pittsburgh Weekly Gazette* 58 (15 September 1843): 3, in Jessee, ed., *Papers of Joseph Smith,* 1:438–44.

upbraideth not." I just determined I'd ask him. I immediately went out into the woods where my father had a clearing, and went to the stump where I had stuck my axe when I had quit work, and I kneeled down, and prayed, saying, "O Lord, what Church shall I join?" Directly I saw a light, and then a glorious personage in the light, and then another personage, and the first personage said to the second, "Behold my beloved Son, hear him." I then, addressed this second person, saying, "O Lord, what Church shall I join." He replied, "don't join any of them, they are all corrupt." The vision then vanished, and when I come to myself, I was sprawling on my back; and it was some time before my strength returned. When I went home and told the people that I had a revelation, and that all the churches were corrupt, they persecuted me, and they have persecuted me ever since. They thought to put me down, but they hav'nt succeeded, and they can't do it."

## Alexander Neibaur, 1844

A Jewish German, Alexander Neibaur was among the early converts to join the Church in Preston, England, where he had migrated from his native land to practice dentistry. Neibaur and his family migrated again to Nauvoo in the early 1840s, where he became an associate of Joseph Smith. In May 1844 Neibaur was present at a small gathering to which Joseph gave an account of his vision just a month before he was murdered. Recording in broken English, Neibaur wrote in his journal of hearing Joseph relate the vision (see Plate 18).[18]

---

18. Alexander Neibaur, Journal, 24 May 1844, Church History Library.

## Transcription of Alexander Neibaur, 1844 Account

Br Joseph tolt us the first call he had a Revival meeting his mother & Br & Sist got Religion, he wanted to get Religion too wanted to feel & ~~sho~~ shout like the Rest but could feel nothing, opened his Bible ~~f~~ the first Passage that struck him was if any man lack wisdom let him ask of God who giveth to all men liberallity & upbraidat[h] not went into the Wood to pray kneelt himself down his tongue was closet cleavet to his roof—could utter not a word, felt easier after a while = saw a fire towards heaven came near & nearer saw a personage in the fire light complexion blue eyes a piece of white cloth drawn over his shoulders his right arm bear after a wile a other person came to the side of the first Mr Smith then asked must I join the Methodist Church = No = they are not my People, ~~all~~ have gone astray there is none that doeth good no not one, but this is my Beloved son harken ye him, the fire drew nigher Rested upon the tree enveloped him [page torn] comforted Indeavoured to arise but felt uncomen feeble = got into the house told the Methodist priest, [who] said this was not a age for God to Reveal himself in Vision Revelation has ceased with the New Testament.

With these documents, a seeker has access to the entire known historical record that relates directly to the contemporary descriptions of Joseph Smith's first vision. One might assume that all readers would arrive at exactly the same conclusions about what these documents mean or how they should be understood. But such an assumption would be wrong.

CHAPTER 5

# Three Critiques of Joseph Smith's Testimony

---

Books, articles, and numerous Internet websites work to undermine faith in Joseph Smith's first vision, but historically there have been just three main arguments against it. The minister to whom Joseph reported the event responded that there were no such things these days. More than a century later and in a literary style that masked her weakness in following the historical method, Fawn Brodie wrote that Joseph invented the vision years after he said it happened. A generation later, Wesley Walters charged Joseph with inventing revivalism when, Walters claimed, a lack of historical evidence proved that there was none and therefore there was no subsequent vision as a result. By now it has become a foregone conclusion for some that there are no such things as visions, that Joseph failed to mention his experience for years, and that he then gave conflicting accounts that failed to match historical facts.[1] But these three claims assume much more than they prove.

Each of the three arguments begins with the conclusion that

---

1. Dan Vogel, *Joseph Smith: The Making of a Prophet* (Salt Lake City: Signature, 2004), xv.

the vision simply could not have happened as Joseph described it. Philosophers describe that kind of premise as *a priori,* a Latin term that describes knowledge that is, essentially, assumed. In other words, *a priori* knowledge does not rely on experience for verification. It is based on definitions, widely shared beliefs, and reason. Knowledge derived from experience is *a posteriori.* Joseph testified that he experienced a divine revelation and therefore knew. The epistemology in Joseph's first vision accounts is *a posteriori.* The epistemology of Joseph's vision critics is *a priori.* They know that what Joseph said happened could not have happened because all reasonable people know that such things do not happen.

### "No Such Thing As Visions"

"Some few days after I had this vision," Joseph reported, "I happened to be in the company with one of the Methodist preachers" who had contributed to the religious fervor. "I took occasion to give him an account of the vision," Joseph continued, "I was greatly surprised at his behavior; he treated my communication not only lightly but with great contempt, saying it was all of the devil, that there were no such things as visions or revelations in these days; that all such things had ceased with the apostles, and that there never would be any more of them."[2]

The preacher's premises were all *a priori,* namely—

- Joseph's story was of the devil.
- There were no such things as revelations in what Charles Dickens called the age of railways.

---

2. See Joseph's 1838 account in chapter 4.

- Visions or revelations ceased with the apostles of Christ's time.
- There would never be any more revelation.

No doubt this good fellow was sincere in each of these beliefs and striving as best he knew to prevent Joseph from becoming prey to fanaticism. But he did not know from experience the validity of any of the four premises he set forth as positive facts. All he knew *a posteriori* is that he himself had not had a vision or a revelation. On what basis, then, could this minister evaluate Joseph's claims and make such sweeping statements?

An answer to that question lies in understanding the pressures on a Methodist minister in Joseph's area in 1820. Joseph did not name the minister to whom he reported the vision. It's not clear whether it was George Lane, whom Joseph's brother William and Oliver Cowdery credited with awakening Joseph spiritually. Joseph could have heard or visited with Reverend Lane one or more times during his ministry in Joseph's district in 1819 and the early 1820s, as he frequently visited the area from his home in Pennsylvania.[3] There were local Methodist ministers, any one of whom Joseph could have told of his experience. All of them were conscious that Methodism was tending away from the kind of spiritual experiences Joseph described and toward a more respectable, reasonable religion. John

---

3. *The Latter Day Saints' Messenger and Advocate* (December 1834): 42; William Smith, *William Smith on Mormonism* (Lamoni, Iowa, 1883), 6; *Deseret Evening News* (Salt Lake City, Utah), 20 January 1894, 11; Larry C. Porter, "Reverend George Lane—Good 'Gifts,' Much 'Grace,' Marked 'Usefulness,'" *BYU Studies* 9, no. 3 (Spring 1969): 321–40.

Wesley, the founder of Methodism, had worried that Methodists would multiply exponentially in number only to become "a dead sect, having the form of religion without the power."[4] And Methodism indeed grew abundantly because it took the claims of people like Joseph so seriously. Its preachers encouraged personal conversions that included intimate experiences with God, including visions and revelations. But then, as John Wesley had worried, Methodism became less welcoming to such manifestations.[5] Just as Joseph was coming of age, many leaders of Methodism were becoming embarrassed by what respectable people regarded as its excesses. Methodism had risen to meet the needs of the many people who could not find a church that took their spiritual experiences seriously. But with its phenomenal growth came a shift from the margin to the mainstream.

Joseph was likely naïve about that shift, which is easier to see historically than it was at the time. Probably all Joseph knew is that he had caught a spark of Methodism and wanted to feel the same spiritual power as the persons he saw and heard at the meetings. He finally experienced that power in the woods, as so many Methodist converts, encouraged by their preachers, appeared to have done before him. So it was

---

4. John Wesley, "Thoughts upon Methodism," in *The Methodist Societies: History, Nature, and Design,* ed. Rupert E. Davies, in *The Bicentennial Edition of the Works of John Wesley,* ed. W. Reginald Ward and Richard P. Heitzenrater (Nashville, Tenn.: Abingdon, 1989), 9:527.

5. Christopher C. Jones, "The Power and Form of Godliness: Methodist Conversion Narratives and Joseph Smith's First Vision," *Journal of Mormon History* 37, no. 2 (Spring 2011): 88–114; Jon Butler, *Awash in a Sea of Faith: Christianizing the American People* (Cambridge: Harvard University Press, 1990), 241. See John H. Wigger, *Taking Heaven by Storm: Methodism and the Rise of Popular Christianity in America* (Urbana and Chicago: University of Illinois Press, 1998), chapter entitled "Methodism Transformed."

shocking to him when the minister reacted against what Joseph assumed would be welcome news.

As for the minister, he may have heard messages in Joseph's story in ways that led him to respond negatively, especially if Joseph told the part about learning that religious professors spoke well of God but denied his power. No Methodist minister wanted to hear that the fear of his denomination's founder had been realized. Yet by 1820 many Methodists were concerned about what had for nearly two hundred years been termed *enthusiasm,* "derived from Greek *en theos,* meaning to be filled with or inspired by a deity."[6] To be accused of enthusiasm in Joseph Smith's world was not a compliment. It meant that one was perceived as mentally unstable and irrational. Methodists had tried to walk a fine line between valuing authentic spiritual experience, yet stopping well short of enthusiasm. It seems likely that young Joseph was not attuned to the sophisticated difference that had been worked out by Methodist theologians. He reported to the minister what he thought would be a highly valued experience that seemed to resemble the experiences of other sincere Christians. But his experience was received as an embarrassing example of enthusiasm and thus condemned.

## Invention and Embellishment

Fawn Brodie largely shaped the skeptical interpretations of Joseph's first vision. She first articulated major criticisms that others have since adopted and published and that circulate widely today. In the first edition of her biography of Joseph,

---

6. Ann Taves, *Fits, Trances, & Visions: Experiencing Religion and Explaining Experience from Wesley to James* (Princeton: Princeton University Press, 1999), 17.

published in 1945, Brodie cited his 1838 history, the one excerpted in the Pearl of Great Price. She reported that her efforts to research at the Church archives were thwarted.[7] She tried but could not access Joseph's 1832 diary. She did not draw on Joseph's 1835 journal or the 1832 account in Joseph's Letterbook. She therefore concluded that no one had spoken of the vision between 1820 and about 1840. She interpreted the limited evidence to mean that Joseph concocted the vision in the wake of an 1837 banking crisis "when the need arose for a magnificent tradition."[8]

Fawn Brodie did not change her assumptions when she revised her biography of Joseph after the 1832 and 1835 accounts were discovered and published. She did not reconsider her interpretation in the light of evidence that showed Joseph had written and spoken openly of the vision on more than one occasion earlier than 1838. Rather, with characteristic insinuation, she simply substituted *1830* for *1834* in this sentence about the vision: "It may have been sheer invention, created some time after 1830 when the need arose for a magnificent tradition."[9] She also noted in her second edition the differences in details between the accounts, suggesting that their inconsistencies evidenced Joseph's invention and embellishment of the story.

Fawn Brodie persuaded her publisher by emphasizing her "attitude of complete objectivity," but privately she knew of her

---

7. Newell G. Bringhurst, *Fawn McKay Brodie: A Biographer's Life* (Norman: University of Oklahoma Press, 1999), 84–85.

8. Fawn M. Brodie, *No Man Knows My History: The Life of Joseph Smith the Mormon Prophet* (New York: Alfred A. Knopf, 1945), 25.

9. Fawn M. Brodie, *No Man Knows My History: The Life of Joseph Smith the Mormon Prophet* 2d ed. (New York: Vintage, 1995), 25.

psychological need to understand Joseph's life and escape his influence. She reflected that writing the book enabled her to assert her independence. She called it a "compulsion to liberate myself wholly from Mormonism." She decided in the process of preparing the biography to see in the historical facts evidence that Joseph had consciously concocted the vision with intent to deceive. Having read an early draft of her biography, a close confidant wrote that he was "particularly struck with the assumption your MS makes that Joseph was a self-conscious imposter." Though sympathetic to her work, this advisor worried about what he called her "bold judgments on the basis of assumptions." A later reviewer noted similarly that she regularly stated "as indisputable facts what can only be regarded as conjectures supported by doubtful evidence."[10]

It is not hard to sympathize with Fawn Brodie. Having been raised as a Latter-day Saint, she chose to leave the faith and underwent a painful reorientation process that required her to reinterpret Joseph Smith's first vision. None of us is so very different from her in that our identities and psychologies are bound up in our various commitments. We cannot escape Joseph Smith's first vision any more than she could, and we work to make sense of the evidence for ourselves in ways that are satisfying to our intellects and to our souls. But whatever her motives and our efforts to sympathize, it is Brodie's method that concerns us here. Critical interpretations of Joseph's vision, such as hers, share a common hermeneutic or explanatory method. They *assume* how a person in Joseph's position, or persons in

---

10. Bringhurst, *Fawn McKay Brodie*, 80, 87, 95, 105, 115.

his neighborhood, would have acted if his story were true and then show that his accounts vary from the assumed scenarios. They usually postulate a hypothetical alternative to Joseph's own explanation.[11]

## Anachronistic Critique

That is what Wesley Walters did. He originated the persistent argument that Joseph's canonized first vision account is anachronistic, or out of historical order. He was pastor of the United Presbyterian Church in Marissa, Illinois, when he published in the fall of 1967 an innovative article that asserted there was no evidence of religious revival in Palmyra, New York, in the spring of 1820, and therefore Joseph's claim to have been influenced by such religious fervor must be false.[12] Richard Bushman said that Walters "performed a very positive service to the cause of Mormon History because he was a delver. He went deep into the heart of the archives. And Mormons had accepted a lot of things as simple facts—for example, that there was a revival in Joseph Smith's neighborhood around the 1820 period."[13] Walters noted accurately that before his work Mormon scholars had "*assumed* that Joseph Smith's account must be correct."[14] According to Bushman,

---

11. Bringhurst, *Fawn McKay Brodie*, 106.
12. Wesley P. Walters, "New Light on Mormon Origins from Palmyra Revival," *Bulletin of the Evangelical Theological Society* 10, no. 4 (1967): 227–44; repr., *Dialogue* 4, no. 1 (1969): 60–67.
13. Richard L. Bushman, interview by Samuel Dodge, 31 July 2009, Provo, Utah, transcription in possession of the author.
14. Walters, "New Light on Mormon Origins," *Dialogue* 4, no. 1 (1969): 61.

Reverend Walters "made us realize that we can't assume anything. Everything had to be demonstrated and proved."[15]

That realization led Truman Madsen and the Institute of Mormon Studies at Brigham Young University to sponsor a team of talented, well-educated young Mormon historians to research all the evidence they could find.[16] Their research shows clearly that there are two main weaknesses in the Walters argument, namely, the fallacies of negative proof and of irrelevant proof. Historian David Hackett Fischer defined the fallacy of negative proof as "an attempt to sustain a factual proposition merely by negative evidence. It occurs whenever a historian declares that there is no evidence that X is the case and then proceeds to affirm or assume that not-X is the case."[17] Walters argued creatively that "a vision, by its inward, personal nature, does not lend itself to historical investigation," but "a revival is a different matter." He posited, therefore, that he could disprove Joseph's claim to a vision by showing that "in 1820 there was no revival in any of the churches in Palmyra and its vicinity."[18] He erred against the historical method by arguing, in other words, that a lack of evidence for a Palmyra revival was proof that the vision did not occur.

Reverend Walters also erred in arguing an irrelevant proof. Joseph's accounts do not claim that the revivalism centered in Palmyra itself, as Walters argues, or that the revivalism

---

15. Bushman, interview by Dodge, 31 July 2009.
16. Truman G. Madsen, "Guest Editor's Prologue," *BYU Studies* 9, no. 3 (Spring 1969): 235–40.
17. David Hackett Fischer, *Historians' Fallacies: Toward a Logic of Historical Thought* (New York: Harper, 1970), 47.
18. Walters, "New Light on Mormon Origins," *Dialogue* 4, no. 1 (1969): 61.

occurred in 1820. Rather, Joseph said that the excitement began in the second year after his family moved to Manchester, New York, meaning in 1819, and he located the "unusual excitement on the subject of religion" around Manchester, not Palmyra. Joseph used a Methodist term to describe a wider geographical scope than Walters's emphasis on the village of Palmyra. Joseph said "the whole *district* of country seemed affected" by the revivalism (emphasis added). To nineteenth-century Methodists, a district was somewhat akin to today's Latter-day Saint stake or Catholic diocese. Joseph claimed only that there was unusual religious excitement in the region or district around Manchester that began sometime in 1819, during the second year after his family's move there.[19]

There is evidence that an intense revival stirred Palmyra in 1816–17 when Joseph moved there with his family. It may have catalyzed Joseph's 1832 description of his mind becoming seriously concerned for the welfare of his soul "at about the age of twelve years."[20] In June 1818, according to the biographer of a Methodist minister who was there, a camp-meeting took place in Palmyra that led to the baptism of about twenty people into the Methodist faith while twice that number united with the Methodist Episcopal Church.[21] About that same time Joseph's family purchased a farm in Manchester, about three

---

19. See Joseph's 1838 account in chapter 4.
20. See Joseph's 1832 account in chapter 4.
21. According to E. Latimer, Seager's biographer, the Reverend Aurora Seager wrote in his diary: "I attended a camp-meeting at Palmyra" on 19 June 1818 and reported that over the subsequent few days about twenty people were baptized and forty joined the Methodist Episcopal Church. See E. Latimer, *The Three Brothers: Sketches of the Lives of Rev. Aurora Seager, Rev. Micah Seager, Rev. Schuyler Seager, D.D.* (New York: Phillips & Hunt, 1880), 22.

miles south of Palmyra. The next summer, 1819, Methodists of the Genesee conference assembled at Vienna (now Phelps), New York, within walking distance of the Smiths' new farm. The Reverend George Lane and dozens of other exhorters were present. One participant remembered the result was a "religious cyclone which swept over the whole region."[22] Joseph's contemporary and acquaintance, Orsamus Turner, remembered that Joseph caught a "spark of Methodism" at a meeting along the road to Vienna.[23] A Palmyra newspaper and the diary of a Methodist minister confirm a weekend camp-meeting in Palmyra in June 1820. If he had known about this evidence, given the way he consistently interpreted evidence in support of his conclusion, the Reverend Walters might have objected that a June 1820 camp-meeting would be too late to catalyze Joseph's early spring vision. And if so, he might have been quite right—but not necessarily. It snowed heavily on May 28 that year, and given the realities in that environment, Joseph may have attached a meaning to "early spring" that is different from our assumptions of what that term means. But Joseph's descriptions do not depend on external events in Palmyra or in 1820. The diaries of the Methodist itinerant preacher Benajah Williams evidence that Methodists and others were hard at work in Joseph's district all the while. They combed the countryside and convened camp-meetings to help such unchurched souls as Joseph get religion. The response was phenomenal,

---

22. Quoted in Milton V. Backman Jr., "Awakenings in the Burned-Over District: New Light on the Historical Setting of the First Vision," *BYU Studies* 9, no. 3 (Spring 1969): 308.

23. Orsamus Turner, *History of the Pioneer Settlement of Phelps and Gorham's Purchase* (Rochester: William Alling, 1852), 213.

especially in western New York, the home of one-third of the Presbyterian converts in the United States in 1820. Baptist churches expanded similarly.[24] Methodism expanded most impressively as such traveling preachers as Williams gathered anxious converts.[25]

The Reverend Walters focused on the word *reformation,* used by Oliver Cowdery to describe the scope of the religious excitement, and on the Reverend George Lane, whom both Cowdery and William Smith, Joseph's brother, credited with being "the key figure in the Methodist awakening." Walters discovered "no evidence" for these claims and concluded that none existed, which was an unwise thing to do.[26] Undiscovered evidence is not the same as nonexistent evidence, and when Walters made the bold claim that no evidence existed, researchers quickly set out to see for themselves. Among the several evidences discovered since are Williams's journals. They document much religious excitement in Joseph's district and region of country in 1819 and 1820. They report that Reverend George Lane was indeed in that area in both of those years and that while there in July 1820 he "spoke on Gods method in bringing about Reffermations."[27] Indeed, the Williams diaries attest that not only Lane but many Methodist preachers in

---

24. Jon Butler, *Awash in a Sea of Faith: Christianizing the American People* (Cambridge: Harvard University Press, 1990), 268–69; Backman, "Awakenings in the Burned-Over District," 314–15, 318.

25. John H. Wigger, *Taking Heaven by Storm* (Oxford: Oxford University Press, 1998), 3–6.

26. Walters, "New Light on Mormon Origins," *Dialogue* 4, no. 1 (1969): 62, 76.

27. Diaries of Benajah Williams, in possession of Michael Brown, Philadelphia, Pennsylvania.

Joseph's time and place created unusual religious excitement, as Joseph described. Writers who have not studied this evidence themselves continue to parrot Walters and the irrelevant claim that "there was no significant revival in or around Palmyra in 1820," but the historical evidence does not contradict Joseph's description.[28]

Though Walters interpreted them otherwise, Joseph's accounts are consistent with the mounting evidence. He said that the unusual religious excitement in his district or region "commenced with the Methodists" and that he "became somewhat partial" to Methodism (Joseph Smith–History 1:5, 8; hereafter cited as JS–H). The Walters thesis, though heartfelt and tenaciously defended by him and uncritically accepted and perpetuated by others, no longer seems tenable or defensible.[29] Walters succeeded in establishing "the fact that his [Joseph's] immediate neighborhood shows no evidence of an 1820 revival" without showing that anything Joseph said was false.[30] Thin evidence for revivalism in Joseph's "neighborhood" or in Palmyra village in 1820 is not evidence that there was not a vision in the woods near Manchester in the wake of well-documented religious excitement "in that region of country."[31]

Latter-day Saint historians of the first vision have credited Walters with motivating them to investigate the context of

---

28. Robert D. Anderson, *Inside the Mind of Joseph Smith: Psychobiography and the Book of Mormon* (Salt Lake City: Signature, 1999), 9.
29. Backman, "Awakenings in the Burned-Over District," 309; Richard L. Bushman, "The First Vision Story Revived," *Dialogue* 4, no. 1 (1969): 85.
30. Walters, "New Light on Mormon Origins," *Dialogue* 4, no. 1 (1969): 69.
31. See Joseph's 1838 account in chapter 4.

Joseph's accounts, but they fault him for forcing his thesis.[32] We can easily understand his determined efforts and unwillingness to give up his point, however. Joseph's most definitive account of his vision relates how he told his mother, "I have learned for myself that Presbyterianism is not true" (JS–H 1:20). He also quoted the Savior as saying that the Christian creeds "were an abomination" (JS–H 1:19). Latter-day Saints who feel defensive about the reverend's efforts to discredit the vision should be able to sympathize with his response to Joseph's testimony. In one sense, his determined and enduring devotion to his cause is admirable. Even so, his arguments are not as airtight as they may seem, and his evidence, or lack thereof, does not prove what he claims it does.

Similarly, the critics' *a priori* certainty that the vision never happened as Joseph said it did is not a proven historical fact based on the testimony of witnesses or on hard data. Rather, those determined beliefs reflect each critic's heartfelt, reasoned belief about what is possible. Their commitment to skepticism about the kind of supernatural events Joseph described prevents them from believing in the possibilities that the historical accounts offer. In other words, all of the unbelieving explanations share a common interpretive method, sometimes called the hermeneutic of suspicion, which in this case simply means interpreting Joseph Smith's statements skeptically, unwilling to trust that he might be telling the truth. One historian who

---

32. Dean C. Jessee and James B. Allen, 27 July 2009; Richard L. Anderson, 29 July 2009; Larry Porter, 30 July 2009; Richard L. Bushman, 31 July 2009; Milton V. Backman Jr., 12 August 2009; interviews by Samuel Dodge; transcriptions in possession of the author.

does not believe Joseph Smith said that he couldn't trust the accounts of the vision because they were subjective and that it was his job to figure out what really happened. But how will this skeptical scholar discover what actually happened when he is unwilling to trust the only eyewitness or the process of personal revelation? Such historians assume godlike abilities to know, yet they don't trust God's ability to reveal truth or theirs to receive it. They don't seem to grasp the profound irony that they are replacing the subjectivity of historical witnesses with their own. I call their method subjectivity squared. They dismiss the historical documents and severely limit possible interpretations by predetermining that Joseph's story is not credible. When Joseph's 1832 account was discovered in the 1960s, opening to Fawn Brodie interpretive possibilities different from her original thesis, she did not respond with willingness to consider that Joseph might be telling the truth but simply fitted the new evidence into her previous conclusion. And because the evidence is now more abundant than ever, parts of Fawn Brodie's thesis are not as compelling as they once were. The evidence she analyzed in her second edition suggested to her that Joseph embellished each telling of the vision until it matured into the canonized 1838–39 account. But later accounts do not continue to become longer, more detailed, or elaborate. Rather, these accounts return to sounding like Joseph's earlier, less-developed accounts. This evidence can be interpreted as Joseph's intention to make his 1838 account definitive and developed for publication, whereas some of the less-developed accounts, including ones later than 1838, were created for other purposes. Some were delivered on the spur of the moment and captured by someone remembering and writing later.

The discovery of considerable evidence of revivalism in both 1819 and 1820 in and around Palmyra, and especially in the broader "region" Joseph described, did not alter the argument Wesley Walters continued to make. No matter what evidence came to light, he interpreted it according to his original conclusion. He chose not to see the possibilities available to those who approach Joseph's accounts on a quest to discover if he could possibly be telling the truth.

Sometimes, in an effort to defend their faith, Latter-day Saints have responded with hostility to the critics of Joseph's vision. If there ever was an appropriate time for such a spirit, it has now passed. We are removed enough that we can respond less defensively and try instead to meet the needs of seekers that may include "those who are in the middle who are trying to decide."[33] I disagree with the *a priori* assumptions and historical interpretations of Fawn Brodie, Reverend Walters, and the Methodist minister who reproved Joseph, but I sympathize with them. I might well have responded as they did if I were in different circumstances. Indeed, the minister's response and the reverend's are not so different from many LDS defenses of faith. Each of the critics is a child of God who is inherently valuable and interesting. They are vulnerable personalities, like the rest of us. They worked hard to figure out how to relate to Joseph Smith's first vision. I wish to treat them as I would like to be treated by them and as Joseph taught the Relief Society

---

33. Bushman, interview by Dodge, 31 July 2009.

sisters in Nauvoo: "The nearer we get to our heavenly Father, the more are we dispos'd to look with compassion on perishing souls—to take them upon our shoulders and cast their sins behind our back.... If you would have God have mercy on you, have mercy on one another."[34]

---

34. Discourse, 9 June 1842, Nauvoo, Illinois, "A Book of Records Containing the Proceedings of the Female Relief Society of Nauvoo," 62, Church History Library, The Church of Jesus Christ of Latter-day Saints, Salt Lake City, Utah. Available online at http://josephsmithpapers.org.

CHAPTER 6

# Listening to Joseph Smith Communicate

⸺⸻⸺

When it comes to Joseph Smith's first vision, learning to seek instead of assume means listening to Joseph communicate what he remembered about his experience. Understanding Joseph requires us to let him explain himself on his terms, not ours. It is common for both believers and critics of Joseph to assume that they know exactly what he meant. Few question the common assumption that Joseph communicated complete, static memories flawlessly and that we receive and understand them that way as well. But such is not the case. Joseph acknowledged that he could not communicate the experience perfectly. He struggled to communicate it at all, and he lacked the ability to express certain aspects that defied description. Rather than assuming that we have perfectly understood Joseph's descriptions, the historical method and the discipline of seeking diligently teach us that we must listen to Joseph extremely carefully in order to recover just his representation of the actual experience. Otherwise we run the risk of impeaching Joseph's testimony when we discover that it does not match unfounded assumptions that are nothing more than hypothetical ideas about what he should have said if his experience were real. Or, even worse, we may fault Joseph for not telling the truth when we fail to listen carefully enough to understand the truth he intended to communicate.

According to Joseph, heavenly beings communicated with him in the woods. He then communicated in several accounts some of what transpired in that event. In any communication an encoder sends the signal and a decoder receives it. "A signal," wrote one communication theorist, "is anything that conveys information."[1] Always there is noise between the sender and the receiver of the signal and it limits and hinders perfect transmission and reception. In terms of communication, noise is not just audible sound. Sound or physical noise can interrupt a signal, but other kinds of noise hinder communication too. Semantic noise happens when the encoder sends signals that the receiver lacks the ability to decipher. Psychological noise happens when a receiver's assumptions or prejudices or preconceived notions or emotions prevent an accurate interpretation of the signal. God may reveal flawless signals, but no mortal, including the youthful Joseph Smith, receives communication flawlessly. There is always noise. And in this case the process of communication is doubly difficult because Joseph's best efforts to recommunicate his experience to us are also compromised by communication noise.

Joseph keenly felt that he lacked the ability to communicate what he had experienced. At about the same time that he composed his earliest account in 1832, he lamented that he

---

1. Bart Kosko, *Noise* (New York: Penguin, 2006), 4.

was confined by what he called "the little narrow prison almost as it were totel darkness of paper pen and ink and a crooked broken scattered and imperfect language."[2] Besides, much of it he simply could not tell. He said that the heavenly beings he witnessed defied description. Shortly before his death, Joseph acknowledged that no one knew his history, despite his numerous attempts to describe it: "I cannot tell it. I shall never undertake it; if I had not experienced what I have I should not have known it myself."[3] So rather than assume that they can know all about the vision by reading Joseph's accounts, seekers recognize that they can understand only some of what Joseph experienced and only as it comes to us through his memory and the limits of communication.

Joseph's vision was a particular kind of communication, namely revelation. "Revelation," according to Elder David A. Bednar, "is communication from God to His children on the earth."[4] Elder Bednar described two types of revelation. One is like turning on a light switch and dispelling darkness in an instant. Joseph's experience in the woods belongs to this category. The other type of revelation is a process, like watching night turn into morning as the rising sun gradually and subtly replaces darkness.[5] The process type of revelation yields insight from ongoing inspiration. This is the kind of revelation

---

2. Joseph Smith to William W. Phelps, 27 November 1832, Church History Library, The Church of Jesus Christ of Latter-day Saints, Salt Lake City, Utah. Available online at http://josephsmithpapers.org.
3. Discourse, 7 April 1844, Nauvoo, Illinois, *Times and Seasons* 5 (15 August 1844): 612–17.
4. David A. Bednar, "The Spirit of Revelation," *Ensign*, May 2011, 87.
5. Bednar, "Spirit of Revelation," 87.

that resulted from Joseph's vision. He accumulated richer and deeper understanding of his vision as he gained subsequent experience and reflected on it. When we listen carefully to Joseph's efforts to communicate, it becomes clear that he related both types of revelation in his several accounts. They tell us how he experienced the vision at the time and how he experienced it again and again over time.

Seekers begin the quest to listen to Joseph by recognizing that his accounts are descriptions of a revelatory event and also, as religion scholar David Carpenter described revelation, "a process mediated through language."[6] The very language whose communicative inadequacies Joseph lamented, in other words, is necessarily the means by which we must receive the signals he sent about the nature of his partly indescribable experience. Seekers find the challenge of listening to Joseph tell his vision both daunting and inviting. Knowing that he had an important story to tell, Joseph was concerned about the limits on his ability to communicate clearly. His earliest known account begins with a disclaimer in which he explains why he felt that his ability to communicate in writing was inadequate. His parents' large family, he said, "required the exertions of all that were able to render any assistance for the support of the Family therefore we were deprived of the bennifit of an education suffice it to say I was mearly instructtid in reading ~~and~~ writing and the ground <rules> of Arithmatic which constuted my whole literary acquirements." In this passage we hear

---

6. David Carpenter, "Revelation in Comparative Perspective: Lessons for Interreligious Dialogue," *Journal of Ecumenical Studies* 29, no. 2 (Spring 1992): 185–86; emphasis in original.

Joseph preparing us for the rough composition of his subsequent narrative. We hear the tension between his knowing that it was vital for him to communicate his singular experience and his sense of inadequacy to communicate it clearly. With that recognition we are prepared to hear Joseph's marvelous story in crooked, broken, scattered, imperfect language. It is a bit like listening to someone communicate in a language they have learned but not yet mastered.

We can also begin listening carefully to Joseph by thinking historically. In other words, we recognize that Joseph's concerns at age fourteen were different from the issues that occupied his mind when he came later to write or dictate the accounts as the adult leader of an expanding church. We will explore ways in which the historical context of each account shaped Joseph's memory of the event and vice versa, but here we are interested in realizing that teenage Joseph was not yet a prophet for others. He was a simple repentant sinner anxiously but unsuccessfully seeking salvation before finally finding Christ's forgiveness, love, and joy for himself. He experienced the reality of a God who was personally responsive to sincere prayers. That is what we hear when we listen to his earliest account.

One of the most striking themes we hear in Joseph's several accounts is his effort to communicate the deep frustration and anxiety he experienced before his vision. In 1832 he clearly communicated his overwhelming concern "for the wellfare of my immortal Soul which led me to searching the scriptures." But his search resulted in "grief" rather than relief, and Joseph became "excedingly distressed" because he knew he needed forgiveness but could not find it. In 1835 Joseph said that he was "wrought up in my mind" and that he considered it crucial to be right "in matters that involve eternal consequ[e]nces." Even so, he was "perplexed in mind." In 1838 Joseph described even further his period of "serious reflection and great uneasiness" as he tried to sort out "the confusion and strife amongst the different denominations." He felt paralyzed and found it "impossible for a person young as I was and so unacquainted with men and things to come to any certain conclusion who was right and who was wrong. My mind at different times was greatly excited for the cry and tumult were so great and incessant." When we listen carefully to Joseph we hear him emphasizing how much he labored "under the extreme difficulties" caused by knowing that he needed forgiveness without being able to find it.

Joseph's vital experience with the Bible is a theme in most of his accounts. The bridge between Joseph's distressed, perplexed, anxious state and his vision was the epiphany that resulted from his reading and reflecting on James 1:5. As Joseph realized the implication of the invitation to ask of God, his outlook changed completely. He had been scouring the Bible for the answer to his question, looking for a passage that would tell him where to find forgiveness. But then he experienced what he called "a realising sense" that the Bible was less an archive of answers than it was a book of examples of people who asked for and received answers directly from God. This realization was part of Joseph's revelatory process. It catalyzed the vision in the woods. Joseph's clear communication of the importance of this preliminary revelation constitutes one of the most impressive passages in any of his accounts:

While I was laboring under the extreme difficulties caused by the contests of these parties of religionists, I was one day reading the Epistle of James, First Chapter and fifth verse which reads, 'If any of you lack wisdom, let him ask of God, that giveth to all men liberally and upbraideth not, and it shall be given him.' Never did any passage of scripture come with more power to the heart of man [than] this did at this time to mine. It seemed to enter with great force into every feeling of my heart. I reflected on it again and again, knowing that if any person needed wisdom from God, I did, for how to act I did not know and unless I could get more wisdom than I then had would never know, for the teachers of religion of the different sects understood the same passage of Scripture so differently as <to> destroy all confidence in settling the question by an appeal to the Bible. At length I came to the Conclusion that I must either remain in darkness and confusion or else I must do as James directs, that is, Ask of God. I at last came to the determination to ask of God, concluding that if he gave wisdom to them that lacked wisdom, and would give liberally and not upbraid, I might venture. So, in accordance with this, my determination to ask of God, I retired to the woods to make the attempt.

When we listen to Joseph carefully, we hear him explain that he saw at least two divine beings in the woods but not necessarily simultaneously. In 1832 he wrote, "the <Lord> opened the heavens upon me and I saw the Lord." His 1838 account says clearly, "I saw two personages" and the 1842 account adds, "two glorious personages." The distinction between the 1832 account's apparent reference to only one being—the

Lord—and the 1838's unequivocal assertion of two beings has led some to wonder and others to criticize Joseph for changing his story. But it may be that we just need to listen more carefully to Joseph tell the story. It may be that we have assumed that we understood his meaning before we did.

Joseph's 1835 account provides the clearest chronology. He said, "A pillar of fire appeared above my head, it presently rested down up me ~~head~~, and filled me with Joy unspeakable, a personage appeard in the midst of this pillar of flame which was spread all around, and yet nothing consumed, another personage soon appeard like unto the first, he said unto me thy sins are forgiven thee." Two of the secondary accounts also say that Joseph first saw one divine personage who then revealed the other. In the 1835 account Joseph also added as an afterthought, "and I saw many angels in this vision." There is nothing in the accounts that requires us to read these variations as exclusive of each other. In other words, there is no reason to suppose that when Joseph says, "I saw two personages," he means that he saw them at exactly the same time for precisely the same length of time or that he did not also see others besides the two. Moreover, because the 1835 account and two of the secondary statements assert that Joseph saw one being who then revealed the other, we could interpret the 1832 account to mean that Joseph saw one being who then revealed another while referring to both beings as "the Lord": "the <Lord> opened the heavens upon me and I saw the Lord." We cannot be sure but it seems plausible that Joseph struggled in 1832 to know just what to call the divine personages. Notice that the first instance of the word *Lord* was inserted into the sentence after the original flow of words, as if Joseph did not know quite how to identify the Being. In 1842 Joseph said that he "saw two glorious personages who exactly resembled each other in features, and likeness." It is plausible that he meant all along to communicate that he envisioned a divine being who revealed another one but that he struggled to characterize them precisely from what he called his narrow prison of paper, pen, and ink. They defied description, after all.

When we listen to Joseph carefully we also hear his subtle but significant distinction between his mind and his heart. Introspective Joseph reflected carefully and wrote quite precisely about his thought processes as well as his emotional responses, but not all of his readers listen carefully enough to discern the difference. It was, according to Joseph, his mind that was worked up as he rationally looked for evidence of "who was right and who was wrong." In 1832 Joseph said that he was about twelve when his "mind became seriously imprest" regarding the welfare of his soul. Each of his accounts narrates a struggle between his head and his heart. He felt deep emotional desires for God's love and forgiveness and attention. But his accounts describe his simultaneous efforts to discern authentic answers through rational processes. Failing to pick up on Joseph's distinction or to understand the tension between head and heart that is the key conflict in his accounts, some readers have wondered or have even been critical of what they regard as inconsistency in Joseph, especially in his 1838 account. There he said that he had often thought about which church was right and that they might all be wrong and wondered how he could know. Later in the same account Joseph acknowledged that he asked the divine beings which church was right because, as he put it, "At this time it had never entered into my *heart* that all were wrong." When we listen carefully to Joseph, we hear him describing the tension between what he had often thought in his head and what he would allow himself to conclude in his heart. His rational processes had suggested repeatedly that all the churches might be wrong, but that was a thought too terrible for Joseph to let sink into his hopeful heart. Emotionally it was such an awful conclusion to the pre-vision teenager that he refused to let the recurring idea become a conclusion without more wisdom from God. What seems to some like inconsistency in Joseph's story can be interpreted as the very point he intended to communicate, namely that his head and his heart were at odds and he desperately needed wisdom from God in order to discern which, if either, he should favor.

CHAPTER 7

# Listening to Joseph Smith Remember

Joseph Smith related several accounts of the vision that were recorded at different times by various writers as he matured and reflected. Some have naturally wondered how certain we can be that Joseph described the vision the way he had experienced it.[1] But rather than seek answers to these good questions about Joseph's memory of his experience, some simply assume that they already know. Common assumptions include the ideas that memory fades over time and that memories, especially of something as momentous as a heavenly vision, are static pictures of the past frozen in time. Let us consider what it means to listen to Joseph communicate his memories

What about Joseph's memory? Is it reliable? The answer, as it turns out, is not simply yes or no. It is both. Remembering is much more complex than many assume. To assume that a person's memory is either reliable or unreliable is to create a logical fallacy called a false dilemma. Memories of our past "include predictable distortions," so much so that one scholar of

---

1. See, for example, Dan Vogel, *Joseph Smith: The Making of a Prophet* (Salt Lake City: Signature, 2004), xv.

memory described them as "true but inaccurate." But he also concluded, based on his experiments, that "it is not the case that the meaning around which autobiographical memory is organized is a complete fabrication of life events. There is a fundamental integrity to one's autobiographical reflections."[2] Joseph's accounts of his vision acknowledge that his memory of his experience was both limited and accurate. He declared, for instance, that he had indeed seen a vision but he estimated the dates of his family's moves, his age at the time of the vision, and the date on which it occurred as if his memory of those peripheral details was less precise.

Seekers strive to understand the dynamics of memory in order to listen more carefully to Joseph communicate his memories. Not simply the storage and retrieval of information, memory is "much more often a reconstruction than a reproduction."[3] What one remembers depends not only on the external event but on the choices one makes about it. Furthermore, memory is an active process in which a person continuously selects, interprets, and integrates what is remembered. In short, Joseph's accounts of his first vision represent the event as he experienced it, both at the time and over time. Such is the power and process of human memory.

Memory begins with an enormous capacity to perceive massive amounts of information for a moment. But as soon as we choose to focus on a tiny slice of the available stimuli, the

---

2. C. R. Barclay, "Schematization of Autobiographical Memory," in D. C. Rubin, ed., *Autobiographical Memory* (Cambridge: Cambridge University Press, 1986), 97.

3. D. C. Rubin, ed., *Autobiographical Memory* (Cambridge: Cambridge University Press, 1986), 4.

rest irretrievably vanishes. When we decide to pay attention to something, memory becomes a conscious, active, or working storehouse that has limited capacity and deteriorates quickly. Most memory evaporates, but when we focus on something repeatedly, it is processed into a secondary memory. Secondary memories do not deteriorate just because time passes, as many assume. Rather, the more thoroughly we process information at the time, the more meaningful and memorable the information becomes. Psychologists and neuroscientists confirm that "memory begins with an emotional association" and that "emotionally intense events produce vivid memories."[4] When we process an event deeply, it endures in our long-term memory indefinitely.

One kind of long-term memory happens when we are conscious that we are in fact remembering. This kind of memory can recall general knowledge without any associated memory of how we know it, as when we remember our name or the color blue. But this conscious kind of memory also recalls specific events of our past and therefore associates knowledge we have gained with the experience that caused us to gain it. In other words, this type of memory includes our own personal history. It is easy to unconsciously blend the two kinds of conscious memories, since we often fill in the gaps of our personal histories with things we assume or remember without knowing exactly how. We can consciously remember some specific components of an event while unconsciously filling in details

---

4. Edmund Blair Bolles, *Remembering and Forgetting: An Inquiry into the Nature of Memory* (New York: Walker, 1988), 29; Sandra Aamodt and Sam Wang, *Welcome to Your Brain* (New York: Bloomsbury, 2008), 101.

with other memories. For this and other reasons, our memories of our past are not fully and completely accurate or inaccurate; they are both. One scholar of memory observed that the people he studied "retained the general meaning of their experiences, even though they were wrong about many particulars."[5]

The memories that compose our personal histories are of two even more specific types: factual and interpretive. Factual memories are of sights, sounds, and so forth. Interpretive memories give meanings to these facts. Factual memory recalls and recognizes. Interpretive memory organizes and provides meaning to otherwise meaningless data. Factual memory could be described as objective—the recall of information "external to the mind"—while interpretive memory is subjective. It is unique to the person remembering.[6] Two people with great memories could sit side-by-side while enjoying a Shakespearean play, a concert, or a sporting event. They would share factual memories of certain sights, sounds, and information that they both observed, but they would each have unique interpretive memories of what they felt or thought or understood about what they shared in common.

Interpretive memories grow and change over time because they are shaped by events subsequent to the episode being remembered. Our present circumstances influence the nature and retrieval of the memory of our past. In the case of Joseph's first vision accounts, his thoughts and circumstances at the time of remembering, telling, recording, and transmitting his

---

5. Barclay, "Schematization," in Rubin, *Autobiographical Memory*, 97.
6. Bolles, *Remembering and Forgetting*, 58, 64–65.

memories undoubtedly shaped what he remembered. "Just as visual perception of the three-dimensional world depends on combining information from the two eyes," wrote one respected psychologist of memory, "perception in time—remembering—depends on combining information from the present and the past."[7]

Joseph Smith's accounts of his first vision abound with these attributes of memory. They are richly descriptive of his mental world, saturated with thoughtful words and deeply emotional phrasing. His recollections of thoughts are so vivid precisely because his "feelings were deep."[8] His narrative descriptions of his experience are journeys inside his own *mind*, a word he used frequently when recounting his experience. In the passages that follow, he carefully describes his state of mind as he reflected on his frustrated search for salvation. In his own hand, he wrote:

> At about the age of twelve years my mind became seriously imprest with regard to the all importent concerns for the wellfare of my immortal Soul which led me to searching the scriptures believeing as I was taught, that they contained the word of God thus applying myself to them and my intimate acquaintance with those of different denominations led me to marvel excedingly . . . thus from the age of twelve years to fifteen I pondered many things in my heart concerning the situation of the world of mankind the contentions and divi[si]ons the wicke[d]ness and abominations

---

7. Daniel L. Schacter, *Searching for Memory: The Brain, the Mind, and the Past* (New York: Basic Books, 1996), 28.
8. See Joseph's 1838 account in chapter 4.

and the darkness which pervaded the ~~of the~~ minds of mankind my mind become excedingly distressed for I become convicted of my sins and by searching the scriptures I found that ~~mand~~ <mankind> did not come unto the Lord but that they had apostatised from the true and liveing faith.⁹

In 1838 Joseph dictated his most definitive account of his experience, again emphasizing awareness of his thoughts and feelings:

> During this time of great excitement my mind was called up to serious reflection and great uneasiness, but though my feelings were deep and often pungent [poignant]. . . . But in process of time my mind became somewhat partial to the Methodist sect, and I felt some desire to be united with them, but so great was the confusion and strife amongst the different denominations that it was impossible for a person young as I was and so unacquainted with men and things to come to any certain conclusion who was right and who was wrong. My mind at different times was greatly excited for the cry and tumult were so great and incessant.¹⁰

Scholars of memory and of religious experiences pay particular attention when people tell of their experiences with awareness that they were aware at the time of the experience. They use the term *meta-awareness* to describe this kind of experience. From the passages quoted above and similar passages of his first vision accounts, we can see that Joseph's awareness

---

9. See Joseph's 1832 account in chapter 4.
10. See Joseph's 1838 account in chapter 4.

that he was aware characterized his experience in the woods and his memories of it.

Joseph's memories seem especially keen when they recall thoughts and the strong emotions he associated with them, as in his description in his 1832 autobiography: "my mind become excedingly distressed"; or in his 1838 history's combination of "serious reflection and great uneasiness." His 1832 account says that his mind became "seriously imprest with regard to the all important concerns for the welfare of my immortal soul," that denominational strife made him grieve and "marvel exceedingly"; that as he "pondered" he became "exceedingly distressed," "felt to mourn," and finally "cried unto the Lord for mercy" and experienced a vision that filled his soul with love for days and led him to "rejoice with great Joy." A November 1835 entry in Joseph's journal says that he was "wrought up in [his] mind" and "perplexed in mind" and describes his increasing hope in the possibility of a heavenly answer and his "fixed determination to obtain" one. His 1838 history recalls "laboring under the extreme difficulties caused" by competing doctrines.[11]

All of Joseph Smith's accounts suggest that he processed his experience deeply and thus memorably. One of his most consistent and vivid memories is his epiphany while reading James 1:5. In his 1838 history, Joseph differentiated how that scripture affected his heart, where it entered with "power" and "great force," and his mind, where he "reflected on it again and

---

11. See Joseph's accounts in chapter 4.

again."¹² Intense emotion and repeated reflection combined, as scholars of memory have learned to expect, to form a vivid, enduring memory.

Joseph's 1842 account for an influential Chicago editor, John Wentworth, contains a clue that suggests how his memory transitioned from sensory perception to short-term to long-term memory. "While fervently engaged in supplication," he said, "my mind was taken away from the objects with which I was surrounded, and I was enwrapped in a heavenly vision."¹³ Memory scholars have noticed that experiences like the one Joseph described here tend to "narrow the focus of attention, leading to improved memory for central details of the target event but impaired memory for peripheral details."¹⁴ Thus, as the vision opened, Joseph focused, quickly losing the ability to recall anything about the environment (except what he may have filled in unconsciously from other memories) but gaining the ability to recall what he envisioned and heard. As much of that peripheral memory subsequently decayed, he could indefinitely recall the most riveting parts of the experience.

The interpretive aspects of Joseph Smith's accounts describe memories that were catalyzed and shaped by his present concerns and circumstances. His 1832 history, almost certainly written between July and December, followed Sidney Rigdon's outspoken 5 July 1832 declaration among the Saints in

---

12. See Joseph's 1838 account in chapter 4.
13. See Joseph's 1842 account in chapter 4, which was first published as "Church History," *Times and Seasons* 3 (1 March 1842): 706–10.
14. Jonathan W. Schooler and Eric Eich, "Memory for Emotional Events," in Endel Tulving and Ferbus I. M. Craik, eds., *The Oxford Handbook of Memory* (New York: Oxford University Press, 2000), 380.

Kirtland, Ohio, that authority had been taken from the Church and entrusted to him.[15] When Joseph addressed the Saints in Kirtland on 8 July, he confiscated Rigdon's preaching license and asserted that "I myself hold the Keys of this last dispensation and I forever will hold them in time and in eternity."[16] Joseph assigned Frederick G. Williams to Rigdon's former role as scribe. Williams then helped Joseph write his autobiography, which seems to have also been sparked by Joseph's 27 November 1832 revelation, now in Doctrine and Covenants 85, reaffirming the need to write history.[17] So Joseph was probably responding to a revealed command to write history and thinking about Rigdon's claim to priesthood keys when he wrote the first known account of his first vision. That account begins, predictably, with Joseph testifying in his own handwriting that "the Kees of the Kingdom of God [had been] confered upon him" by angels and that there was a "continuation of the blessings of God to him" as opposed to Rigdon's version of events.[18] In the 1832 account, Joseph remembered the vision

---

15. On Rigdon's claim, see Lucy Mack Smith, *Lucy's Book: A Critical Edition of Lucy Mack Smith's Family Memoir,* ed. Lavina Fielding Anderson (Salt Lake City: Signature Books, 2001), 560–64; "Philo Dibble's Narrative," in *Early Scenes in Church History: Four Faith Promoting Classics* (Salt Lake City: Bookcraft, 1968), 74–96. See Reynolds Cahoon Diary, 5–17 July 1832 and Charles C. Rich, "History Charles Coulson Rich," 3–4, Church History Library, The Church of Jesus Christ of Latter-day Saints, Salt Lake City, Utah; hereafter cited as Church History Library.

16. Smith, *Lucy's Book,* 560–64.

17. Joseph Smith to William Phelps, 27 November 1832, in Joseph Smith, *Personal Writings of Joseph Smith,* ed. Dean C. Jessee, 2d ed. (Salt Lake City: Deseret Book, 2002), 285. Available online at http://josephsmithpapers.org.

18. See Joseph's 1832 account in chapter 4. For more context, see Karen Lynn Davidson, David J. Whittaker, Mark Ashurst-McGee, and Richard L. Jensen, eds., *Histories, 1832–1844,* vol. 1 of the Histories series of *The Joseph Smith Papers,* edited by Dean C.

as part of a history designed to emphasize that he held the keys of authority.

Joseph Smith's 1838–39 history begins with another connection between his present concerns and his memory of the vision. The "many reports which have been put in circulation by evil disposed and designing persons" he said, "induced [him] to write this history."[19] In the intensely hostile environment of the 1838 account, Joseph remembered learning that professors of Christianity were corrupt and their creeds abominable to God. But then time and extreme opposition sank deeper into the past, giving Joseph a different perspective.

When he revised his 1838 account a few years later, Joseph's flight from Kirtland, Ohio, the Saints' expulsion from Missouri, and his own painful sojourn in jail at Liberty, Missouri, were a few years behind him, and the Saints were beginning to thrive in comparative peace in Nauvoo, Illinois. They had been blessed by friendly, charitable neighbors in and around Quincy, Illinois, and received a liberal charter from a hospitable Illinois legislature. In that environment Joseph did not include the introduction about "evil disposed and designing" conspirators who were militantly out to get him.[20] Joseph's softening interpretive memory can be seen further a couple of years later in his 1842 account, written for public consumption

---

Jessee, Ronald K. Esplin, and Richard Lyman Bushman (Salt Lake City: Church Historian's Press, 2012), 10.

19. See Joseph's 1838 account in chapter 4. See also Davidson et al., *Histories, 1832–1844*, 204.

20. Compare Joseph's 1838 account in chapter 4 with the circa 1841 revision in Joseph Smith, History, fair copy in the handwriting of Howard Coray, Church History Library. Available online at http://josephsmithpapers.org.

at the request of John Wentworth. There he remembered learning in the vision "that all religious denominations were believing in incorrect doctrines."[21] These memories of the same experience were articulated in circumstances that shaped and reshaped them. The form they took had much to do with how Joseph felt at the time he remembered the event. In 1838 he felt defensive against growing opposition, a few years later he felt renewed, then in 1842 he felt responsive to an open-minded invitation and desired to tell his story to positively influence public opinion rather than to condemn Christianity.

Joseph Smith's accounts of his vision show memory that was simultaneously vivid and vague, even within in a single sentence. His 1832 account says that "at about the age of twelve years my mind become seriously imprest with regard to the all important concerns for the wellfare of my immortal Soul which led me to searching the scriptures." He repeatedly used the word *about* to describe events peripheral to the vision, like his age at the time. In an 1835 account Joseph recorded, "When I called on the Lord in mighty prayer, a pillar of fire appeared above my head, it presently rested down upon me head, and filled me with Joy unspeakable, a personage appeard in the midst of this pillar of flame which was spread all around, and yet nothing consumed, another personage soon appeard like unto the first, he said unto me thy sins are forgiven thee, he testifyed unto me that Jesus Christ is the Son of God; &lt;and I saw many angels in this vision&gt; I was about 14 years old

---

21. See Joseph's 1842 account in chapter 4, which was published originally as "Church History," *Times and Seasons* 3 (1 March 1842): 706–10.

when I received this first communication."[22] Joseph keenly described the parts of the experience that he processed deeply and then added as an afterthought his approximate age as best his vague memory of it could recover. Likewise, in 1838 he remembered that an unusual religious excitement occurred in his region only "sometime in the second year after our removal to Manchester," but he felt sure that it began with the Methodists. He remembered that the vision occurred in the "morning of a beautiful clear day early in the spring of Eighteen hundred and twenty," but apparently he could not recall precisely which day. He noted that after the vision he was "between fourteen and fifteen years of age," which his scribe later qualified further by inserting "or thereabouts."[23]

Joseph's accounts are straightforward and factual, but they are also interpretive. His factual memory of what happened in the grove did not change, but his interpretive memory of what the vision meant expanded with his experience. He understood it better and differently with subsequent experience and reflection. For instance, the vision did not become Joseph's *first*, in his mind, until after he had others. With insight born of changed circumstance and enlarged context, Joseph discovered meanings in his vision that were unavailable to him when it occurred. In his prayer of 1820, for example, Joseph primarily had his own salvation in mind, and his earliest known account of his vision emphasized the personal experience of redemption that resulted. But when he told the story in 1835, Joseph

---

22. See Joseph's 9 November 1835 account in chapter 4.
23. See Joseph's 1838 account in chapter 4.

remembered the vision as the first in a series of revelations that led to the publication of the Book of Mormon. From that perspective Joseph used the word *first* to describe the experience and link it to "revelations he ~~had~~ afterward received."[24] Writing again amidst concerted opposition in 1838, with thousands of Saints from Maine to Indian Territory and others in Great Britain, he described the vision as the beginning of a new gospel dispensation against a background of opposition.

Joseph Smith's accounts of his vision exhibit both factual and interpretive memory.[25] His 1838 account provides the best example of what one memory scholar described as the "transformation of memory from fact to meaning."[26] Joseph began by narrating the facts of his early life and the events that led to and composed his vision. One notices the same straightforward style that characterizes the earlier accounts, but then Joseph begins to muse about the events he has just recalled, identifying and assigning meaning. The word *seems* is an indicator of Joseph's shift from external facts to internal meaning: "It seems

---

24. See Joseph's 9 November 1835 account in chapter 4. For more context, see Dean C. Jessee, Mark Ashurst-McGee, Richard L. Jensen, eds., *Journals, Volume 1: 1832–1839*, vol. 1 of the Journals series of *The Joseph Smith Papers*, edited by Dean C. Jessee, Ronald K. Esplin, and Richard Lyman Bushman (Salt Lake City: Church Historian's Press, 2008), 1:87–88. When interviewed about the accounts of Joseph Smith's first vision, Dean Jessee said, "When we have an experience, we relate it one time, and later on we might see it in a different light due to events that have taken place in our own lives. I think that may have played a part in it also" (interview by Samuel Dodge, 2009, transcript in possession of the author).

25. In fact, as religion scholar Ann Taves has argued about memory plasticity generally, "The composition of multiple narratives of an experience from different points of view is an excellent way to examine how interpretations of an experience develop over time." *Religious Experience Reconsidered* (Princeton: Princeton University Press, 2009), 71.

26. Bolles, *Remembering and Forgetting*, 65.

as though the adversary was aware at a very early period of my life that I was destined to prove a disturber & annoyer of his kingdom, or else why should the powers of Darkness combine against me, why the oppression & persecution that arose against me, almost in my infancy?" What is more, Joseph inserted that thought into the story in 1842 while he was reflecting. It was not included in the record of his 1838 memory.[27] Researchers scouring archives for documentation that Joseph was oppressed and persecuted as an infant are likely to look in vain. The relevant archive is his interpretive memory. To a recollecting thirty-four-year-old Joseph, embroiled in efforts to extradite him to hostile Missouri, the oppression and persecution *seemed* to have lasted for a lifetime.

Joseph Smith's factual memory of rejection by a Methodist preacher activated a fascinating interpretive memory. It can be seen best by noticing his shift away from narrating external facts to a description of how he felt. Remembering in 1838 that he was widely persecuted after his vision, Joseph recounted his "serious reflection" on what he described as a recurring thought that he had attracted so much unsolicited attention though "an obscure boy." He described his "great sorrow" vividly. Yet an observer of the outward scene might not have interpreted these events nearly as intensely as Joseph did. Beside the stinging rejection of the Methodist minister to whom he reported his vision, Joseph's memory of the persecution was vague and notably impersonal. There is very little factual memory aside from

---

27. The insertion is in the handwriting of Willard Richards, in Joseph Smith, Manuscript History, Book A1, Church History Library, 132–33. According to his diary, Richards wrote it on 2 December 1842. See his diary for that date, Church History Library.

the rebuff of the preacher, who in Joseph's memory spoke for everyone else. It felt like everyone was allied against him. In the middle of this interpretive memory, though, Joseph stated a factual one. He declared, as if responding to the preacher, that "it was nevertheless a fact, that I had seen a vision." He then returned to his interpretive mode, telling us candidly that subsequent to the vision itself he found meaning in it by comparing his experience to St. Paul's before Herod Agrippa. Throughout this interpretive section, Joseph interjected factual memory to affirm that his vision was undeniably real.[28]

Joseph discovered meanings in his memories. One scholar observed that "merely to remember something is meaningless unless the remembered image is combined with a moment in the present affording a view of the same object or objects. Like our eyes, our memories must see double; these two images then converge in our minds into a single heightened reality."[29] Another scholar called this "insight."[30] Richard Bushman, a believing biographer of Joseph, further described the process. "When we have a strange experience," he said, "something that is new, we have to understand it in terms of what is old. Events and experiences do not carry their meaning on the surface. We have to look around in the inventory of ideas that we have in order to make sense of what has occurred to us." Joseph had to

---

28. Smith, Manuscript History, Book A1, 4.
29. Roger Shattuck, *Proust's Binoculars: A Study of Memory, Time, and Recognition in À la Recherche du temps perdu* (Princeton: Princeton University Press, 1983), 46–47.
30. Bolles, *Remembering and Forgetting*, 65.

"enlarge his inventories . . . in order to make sense of an experience that he had before."[31]

Joseph Smith's understanding of God and Christ seems to have enlarged with time and experience, affecting how he described his vision. His 1832 account describes how "the <Lord> opened the heavens upon me and I saw the Lord and he spake unto me." An 1835 journal entry describes how he "called on the Lord in mighty prayer," and then one "personage" appeared, followed by another, who testified that Joseph's sins were forgiven and "that Jesus Christ is the Son of God." In his 1838 account, Joseph prayed not to the Lord as in 1832 but explicitly and repeatedly to God before being visited by "two personages," one of whom pointed to the other and said, "This is my beloved Son, Hear him." In 1842 Joseph described his prayer to God and his vision of "two glorious personages who exactly resembled each other in features, and likeness." Some analysts of Joseph's accounts, following Fawn Brodie, interpret Joseph's increasingly specific descriptions as evidence of embellishment.[32] They can just as reasonably be read as evidence of insight. Joseph may have had the factual memory at his disposal all along and yet remained unable to articulate the meanings he would subsequently find in it until further experience equipped him with the ability.[33]

Analyzing Joseph's first vision accounts with an

---

31. Richard L. Bushman, interview by Samuel Dodge, 31 July 2009, Provo, Utah, transcript in possession of the author.
32. Shattuck, *Proust's Binoculars*, 46–47.
33. Bushman, interview by Dodge, 31 July 2009.

understanding of the powers and limits of communication and memory provides some answers to whether and in what ways the accounts are reliable representations of his experience. Joseph created human memories of his first vision and communicated some of them to us via the several accounts. They reveal vivid memories of elements of the experience that deeply impressed him—anxious uncertainty prior to the theophany, the epiphany that resulted from reading and reflecting on James 1:5, the feeling of love and redemption resulting from the theophany, and the reality of the vision itself. Interpretive and introspective memories are present as well. Indeed, the accounts reveal that Joseph consciously interpreted the experience and discovered meanings in it later that were not available at the time it occurred. The accounts are not, by Joseph's acknowledgment, a flawless recreation of the event, nor are they "a complete fabrication of life events."[34] Despite distortions and limits in recounting the experience, Joseph's accounts generally exhibit continuity. Moreover, they communicate to seekers Joseph's memories of how he experienced the vision at the time and how he remembered it over time.

---

34. Barclay, "Schematization," in Rubin, *Autobiographical Memory*, 97.

CHAPTER 8

# Seekers Wanted

———⟶•⟵———

This book was written to provide a context and a community for readers who desire to trust Joseph. The context is the empowering knowledge of the historical method and documents that enables seekers to search for their own informed conclusions about what the documents say and mean. The community is in the awareness I hope to create that I and others are sympathetic fellow seekers. Life as a Latter-day Saint seeker can be lonely. It can seem as though you are unwelcome if you wonder or have doubts or if you are still on a quest for light and knowledge when it seems like so many around you have already arrived. You might feel as if you are under attack or all alone. Joseph Smith experienced similar feelings. He told friends that when, as a youth, he attended revival meetings, he wanted badly to join in the shouts of joy but, he said, I "could feel nothing."[1] And he could not pretend that he felt otherwise. So he kept seeking. But when he finally found his answer, he told an adult authority, only to be rejected and deeply hurt as a

---

1. Alexander Neibaur, Journal, 24 May 1844, entry made just a month before Joseph's death. See the full account in chapter 4.

result. That was no way to treat a seeker who was himself trying to find out who he could trust.

This book began by outlining some basic ideas about what and how we could know when it comes to Joseph Smith's first vision. Reviewing the historical method taught us to take seriously the careful study of all available evidence created by those who experienced the past we seek to understand. But the historical method alone will not satisfy seekers with spiritual longings to know whether God would be as responsive to their cries in the wilderness as he was to Joseph's. Such longings can be satisfied by the ongoing quest of seeking not only by study (the historical method in this case) but by faith—the willingness to trust Joseph Smith and the divine beings who responded to his earnest prayer. Here we will consider what it can mean to seek by study and then examine how and why seekers may be willing to exercise faith in Joseph Smith and in the divine personages of whom his accounts testify.

Joseph's several accounts of his first vision tell a consistent story of anxiety followed by a comforting heavenly vision. It is a historical fact that Joseph's accounts of his vision became more specific over time and that they emphasized different dimensions of his experience. In his earliest autobiography, Joseph did not clearly distinguish between "the Lord" who opened the heavens and "the Lord" who forgave his sins and told him that the churches had gone astray. He wrote simply that "the Lord opened the heavens upon me and I saw the Lord," perhaps referring to two separate heavenly beings each as the Lord but not explicitly describing two personages as his later accounts declare. His 1835 account says that he saw one personage and then another, as well as "many angels." In one account Joseph called the experience his "first visitation of Angels"; in another he "saw two glorious personages."[2] These accounts suggest that in 1832 he was referring to two different beings both as "Lord." He apparently saw one divine being first, who introduced another. He said in 1835: "A pillar of fire appeared above my head; which presently rested down upon me, and filled me with unspeakable joy. A personage appeared in the midst of this pillar of flame, which was spread all around and yet nothing consumed. Another personage soon appeared like unto the first: he said unto me thy sins are forgiven thee."[3] Joseph identified the divine beings later in 1838 when he related that "One of <them> spake unto me calling me by name and said (pointing to the other) 'This is my beloved Son, Hear him.'"[4] Joseph's 1835 and 1838 accounts emphasize opposition from an unseen power. The other accounts do not mention that part of the experience. In the 1832 account, Joseph's scribe Frederick G. Williams inserted a clause saying that Joseph was 16 when the vision came, whereas his 1835 and 1842 accounts as well as an 1843 secondary account all say "about 14" and his 1838 account says "in my fifteenth year," or fourteen years old.

Those are historical facts. They are not disputed by well-informed individuals. It is the decision about what they mean—how the facts should be interpreted—that is continually being contested in books and articles, online, and in the hearts and minds of partisans and seekers. There are sound,

---

2. See Joseph's several accounts in chapter 4.
3. See Joseph's 9 November 1835 account in chapter 4.
4. See Joseph's 1838 account in chapter 4.

intelligible reasons, as we have discussed, why we might expect Joseph's accounts to vary. It is not good seeking to conclude based on nothing more than assumptions that the variations should be interpreted to mean that Joseph was not trustworthy. The limits of communication and the dynamics of memory contributed to the variety in the accounts. Seekers will at least want to be open to these and all other possibilities.

Those who trust Joseph tend to interpret faithfully the historical facts he left us, whereas those who distrust him interpret them skeptically. Skeptics who begin with certainty that the vision never happened as Joseph said it did are unwilling to explore the variety of possibilities that the historical documents offer. Believers who are unwilling to examine all of the evidence prevent themselves from fuller understanding and appreciation of Joseph's experience and are often unaware that they may have unfounded assumptions masquerading as testimony. Ironically, this unexamined sense of certainty makes their faith vulnerable. For some, the unfounded part of their testimony will crumble when eroded by the evidence, leaving them wondering whether any part of their formerly certain knowledge was true after all.

Skeptical interpreters suspect that Joseph was deceived or deceptive or both when he told his story. They decide to interpret the evidence to mean that Joseph was at least unreliable and perhaps even scheming. They have decided to believe that Joseph's story is unbelievable. Trusting interpreters decide to interpret the same evidence differently. They determine that the variability in the accounts makes sense in terms of the particular ways Joseph remembered and related the experience and the diverse settings and circumstances in which his accounts were communicated, recorded, and transmitted. They decide to believe that Joseph's story is believable even if it is remarkable.

For those who choose to read Joseph's accounts with skepticism, the interpretation of choice is likely to remain that Joseph elaborated "some half-remembered dream" or concocted the vision as "sheer invention."[5] One skeptical interpreter assumed that Joseph failed to mention his vision "until years after the event" and then gave "conflicting and anachronistic accounts."[6] Those are not historical facts. They are skeptical assumptions about why we do not have more information than we do, as well as about the fact that Joseph reported that he saw a vision. There are other ways to interpret those facts. We can assume, but we do not know, that Joseph did not tell about the vision to others besides the Methodist minister before 1832. We only know that we do not presently have evidence that he did so. We can assume, but we do not know, that Joseph did not write about the vision before 1832. We only know that we do not presently have evidence that he wrote about it before the brief allusion made in 1830 (see D&C 20:5), followed by his 1832 account.

Seekers discern the difference between historical facts that others can verify and interpretations of those facts that are specific to subjective interpreters. And seekers discern the difference between what is assumed and what is known. Some

---

5. Fawn Brodie, *No Man Knows My History*, 2d ed. (New York: Vintage, 1995), 25.
6. Dan Vogel, *Joseph Smith: The Making of a Prophet* (Salt Lake City: Signature, 2004), xv.

assume that we have access to all Joseph said or wrote. We do not, but even if we did, it would not be sound to assume that it would represent everything he remembered. And even if it were, it would not be wise to assume that it would represent all he experienced. We have the equivalent of a few puzzle pieces and are not able yet to discern exactly how the completed puzzle will look. Seekers would rather acknowledge the missing pieces and actively, if patiently, search for them than pretend to know what they must look like.

One will arrive at the same conclusions as skeptics if one decides to share their assumptions about what the facts mean. But other meanings for the same facts are possible. The danger of close-mindedness is as real for believers as for skeptics. Many believers seem just as likely to begin with assumptions rather than a willingness to go where Joseph's accounts lead them. The reasoning process of many believers is no different from Fawn Brodie's. Some assume, for instance, that Joseph would obviously have told his family of the vision immediately, or written it immediately, that he always understood all of its implications perfectly or consistently through the years, or that he would always remember or tell exactly the same story, or that it would always be recorded and transmitted the same. But none of those assumptions is supported by the historical evidence. Some believers turn into skeptics when they learn of the accounts and find that their hypothetical history—assumptions about what would happen if Joseph told the truth—are not supported by the historical record. This, sadly, is simply trading one set of assumptions for another. It is not the seeker's way. The several scholars who have for decades studied and written about the vision accounts share what one of them described as a hermeneutic of trust.[7] This is not an appeal to their authority but a plea for seekers to follow their example of studying all the evidence carefully, without assuming or rushing to conclusions.

So much is at stake in deciding how to think and feel about Joseph Smith's accounts. Each seeker must decide whether to trust him or not. His testimony is remarkable. Some skeptics would say literally incredible, meaning that Joseph's story cannot be credited as possible. It is just too far from normal experience. Joseph hardly blamed them. "If I had not experienced what I have," Joseph said a few weeks before he was assassinated in 1844, "I should not have known it myself."[8] But another response is, of course his account can be trusted. His family trusted him.[9] Thousands of followers in his lifetime trusted him. Millions trust him today, including the scholars who know the relevant historical record best. Obviously Joseph Smith can be trusted, and there are good reasons to trust him. The question for seekers is, then, will you decide to trust him?

Authentic seeking requires us not only to search the historical record thoroughly but to assess our own souls simultaneously. One way to seek introspectively is to identify and examine assumptions, to be just as vigilant in investigating why

---

7. Richard L. Bushman, interview by Samuel Dodge, 31 July 2009, Provo, Utah, transcription in possession of the author.
8. Joseph Smith, Discourse, 7 April 1844, Nauvoo, Illinois, Thomas Bullock Report, Church History Library, The Church of Jesus Christ of Latter-day Saints, Salt Lake City, Utah; hereafter cited as Church History Library.
9. William Smith, *William Smith on Mormonism* (Lamoni, Iowa: Herald, 1883), 3, 9, quoted in Dan Vogel, comp. and ed., *Early Mormon Documents,* 5 vols. (Salt Lake City: Signature, 1996–2003), 1:493, 496.

we are or are not willing to trust Joseph as we are at assessing whether he is trustworthy. Investigating our assumptions helps us understand why we suppose or believe what we do. There is an often-repeated assumption that if Joseph experienced the vision, he would have written it sooner. But there is no evidence or basis for this conclusion. Rather, Joseph and others left us evidence that he was not a skilled writer and quite reluctant to write. It was at about the same time he wrote his earliest vision account in 1832 that Joseph expressed how he felt imprisoned by what he called the "total darkness of paper, pen and ink."[10] When we think carefully about our assumptions, we become capable of asking better-informed questions. Clearer thinking in light of more evidence, for example, might cause us to wonder not just why Joseph waited so long to write about the vision but, given his historical circumstances and the evidence he left us, why he decided to write about it at all. Whatever questions we ask, seeking by the historical method of study requires that we discover the answers in the evidence created by those who experienced the past, not in a hypothetical history we imagine based on assumptions.

Several similar assumptions need to be more critically examined. Many assume, for instance, that Joseph's experience was singular—that no one else experienced anything like it. But it is an historical fact that people in Joseph's general time and region left accounts of their visionary experiences, including some who testified that they envisioned two divine

---

10. The words were later struck out of the letter. See Joseph Smith to William W. Phelps, 27 November 1832, Church History Library. Available online at http://josephsmithpapers.org/paperSummary/letter-to-william-w-phelps-27-november-1832.

beings.[11] Some skeptical interpreters of this fact decide that it means that Joseph was one among many who thought they were hearing from God as a result of religious fervor in their culture. Believing interpreters can be quite comfortable with that interpretation so long as it does not diminish the authenticity of Joseph's revelation. Joseph himself saw a link between religious fervor and his experience in the grove. And he did not deny that others would or could seek and receive revelations. He did not claim to be the sole recipient of a comforting heavenly vision. Joseph's testimony stands or falls based on whether he told the truth about his experience, which has nothing to do with whether others were experiencing similar things.

The evidence left by visionaries in Joseph's culture suggests that his accounts are remarkable in one way. Other visionaries usually told their experiences in more ambiguous terms that tended to uphold rather than challenge the established creeds.[12] At nearly the same time and in the same region as Joseph's vision, for example, Charles Finney pleaded with God in prayer in the woods. Shortly afterward he experienced a vision of Christ in his law office. He later became one of America's foremost revival preachers, distancing himself from his vision in the process. In time Finney referred to his

---

11. Christopher C. Jones, "The Power and Form of Godliness: Methodist Conversion Narratives and Joseph Smith's First Vision," *Journal of Mormon History* 37, vol. 2 (Spring 2011): 88–114; Richard L. Bushman, "The Visionary World of Joseph Smith," *BYU Studies* 37, no. 1 (1997–98): 183–204; "The 'Prognostication' of Asa Wild," *BYU Studies* 37, no. 3 (1997–98): 223–30.

12. Ann Kirschner, "'Tending to Edify, Astonish, and Instruct': Published Narratives of Spiritual Dreams and Visions in the Early Republic," *Early American Studies: An Interdisciplinary Journal* 1, no. 1 (Spring 2003): 216, 229.

experience simply as a "mental state."[13] In contrast, Joseph put progressively more and more emphasis on the reality of his experience. He recognized that his vision challenged the creeds of Christendom and their professors—those who espoused belief in God but denied his power to communicate directly. Though deeply wounded by their rejection of what was so joyful to him, Joseph was uncompromising about the nature of his experience. "I had actually seen a light," Joseph testified, "and in the midst of that light I saw two Personages, and they did in reality speak to me; and though I was hated and persecuted for saying that I had seen a vision, yet it was true."[14]

Learning to ask seeking questions helps us better analyze historical evidence and our own assumptions, intentions, and desires. It can also help us realize that all of us—believers, skeptics, seekers, and those who are some combination—are ultimately seeking the same thing, namely the security that comes from certainty. Some nineteenth-century revival preachers used a tool they called the mourner's bench and their critics sometimes called the anxious bench. It was often a roughhewn pew in the front of the congregation where salvation seekers were invited to sit while the preacher and others prayed for them to become converted. In one sense we are all candidates for the anxious bench. We are anxiously on a quest for certainty. Often our desire for security and the anxieties resulting from uncertainty incline us to respond to Joseph's testimony as

---

13. Garth M. Rosell and Richard A. G. Dupuis, eds., *The Memoirs of Charles G. Finney: The Complete Restored Text* (Grand Rapids, Mich.: Zondervan, 1989), 23. See fn. 32.

14. See Joseph's 1838 account in chapter 4.

we do. Dogmatism, criticism, seeking—each is a way to seek certainty and the resulting security.

Some seek security in the scientific certainty that comes from knowing facts. Some seek security in dogmatism and defensiveness against anything that might erode their sense of certainty, including historical evidence. Others, the wisest in my estimation, seek to avoid the pitfalls of both kinds of self-centered certainty and put their trust in God to guide them. The first two types assume with certainty that they know more than they actually do. The third type begin by humbly acknowledging that they do not know but would like to, and they go to the source of knowledge to teach them. This kind of seeking requires more patience and perseverance than the other ways. It requires an act of conscious, informed faith not just once but continually to trust. Indeed, seeking is the way to truth that emphasizes a benevolent source of knowledge higher than our own, a God to whom we can turn for peace and revelation.

Seekers are interested in verifying Joseph Smith's accounts as a means to the end of what they ultimately seek. If true, his accounts testify of a loving, responsive God and tell how He can be accessed. Joseph's testimonies are thus not only historical documents to be verified but, from a seeker's perspective, they become models of successfully seeking vital knowledge from God. They show how an anxious, vulnerable soul can make the courageous choice to exercise faith. Sarah Edwards, for example, was a seeker a century before Joseph Smith. She was married to the great Jonathan Edwards, whose most famous sermon emphasized a wrathful God who dangled his subjects over the bottomless pit and remained unresponsive to their desires.[15] Sarah preferred a different conception of God. She had a deep desire to "call God my Father" and wondered whether she accurately could. She sought him in private prayer and felt "the presence of God was so near, and so real, that I seemed scarcely conscious of any thing else. God the Father, and the Lord Jesus Christ, seemed as distinct persons, both manifesting their inconceivable loveliness, and mildness, and gentleness, and their great and immutable love to me." Sarah struggled to communicate, as Joseph would a century later, "the peace and happiness, which I hereupon felt." It "was altogether inexpressible."[16] Latter-day Saint scholar Terryl Givens stated the significance of Sarah's seeking in relationship to Joseph's. "Long before Joseph Smith offered his first prayer," he wrote, "thousands and millions of people must have yearned, as Sarah did, for the assurance that God was not the severe, distant, impersonal deity of Jonathan Edwards, but the kind, loving, and very personal God that Joseph found in the Sacred Grove."[17]

The reality and approachability of this God is reason to verify Joseph Smith's vision accounts. If they are trustworthy, the security we seek is available from the loving God of whom they testify. Joseph entered the grove feeling unique and alone.

---

15. Jonathan Edwards, "Sinners in the Hands of an Angry God," in *The Works of President Edwards with a Memoir of His Life,* ed. Sereno Edwards Dwight, 10 vols. (New York: Carvill, 1830), 7:169, 170, 172.

16. Sarah Edwards, in Dwight, *Works of President Edwards,* 1:172–73; emphasis in original; see also George M. Marsden, *Jonathan Edwards: A Life* (New Haven, Conn.: Yale University Press, 2003), 243–44.

17. Terryl L. Givens, "'Lightning Out of Heaven': Joseph Smith and the Forging of Community," *BYU Studies* 45, no. 1 (2006): 10.

It seemed to his teenage soul as if he were one of few who could not feel what so many others were feeling and rejoice with them. Others, meanwhile, mocked the very possibility of divine revelation, as one skeptical writer of Joseph's era did, lumping any who claimed to have experience with God together with "a great part of mankind, in every age, [who] are pleased with the marvelous. Stories of witchcraft, fairies, hobgoblins, revelations, visions, and trances always excite the attention of the superstitious, gain belief, and afford them unspeakable pleasure."[18] But even as skeptics dismissed supernatural experience as nonsense, Joseph and many other spiritual souls were seeking authentic experience with a responsive God.

Joseph's accounts communicate in his "crooked broken scattered and imperfect language" his testimony that he had such an experience and that it filled him with love.[19] The possibility of experiencing this love is the ultimate reason to seek by study and by faith to know the veracity of Joseph's accounts. In other words, one reason to be courageous enough to exercise faith in the God who revealed himself to Joseph Smith is that He is so beautiful, so lovable and loving. He responds to anxious teenagers, forgives their sins, fills them with love that helps them cope with their fears and frustrations, and causes them to rejoice with great joy. He fills seekers of all times and places with love and happiness. But He asks for faith. To come

---

18. A True Narrative of a Most Stupendous Trance and Vision, Which Happened at Sharon, in Connecticut in January, 1789 (n.p., 1793), 3, 11.
19. Joseph Smith to William W. Phelps, 27 November 1832, Church History Library. Available online at http://josephsmithpapers.org.

to increasing degrees of certainty and security by the ongoing process of study and faith, a seeker must be willing to trust God, "must believe that he is, and that he is a rewarder of them that diligently seek him" (Hebrews 11:6).

# Index

Accounts of First Vision: controversy over, 1–2; 1832 account, *Plates 1–5*, 33–41, 101–4, 109; assumptions on, 3–4; 1835 accounts, *Plates 7–9*, 41–43, 104–5, 109, 113; of Levi Richards, *Plate 17*, 63–64; of Alexander Neibaur, *Plate 18*, 65–66; overview of, 31–33; primary, 32–33; timeline of, 34–36; 1838 account, 45–52, 103, 105–9, 113; 1842 account, 52–54, 103–4, 109; of Orson Pratt, 55–59; of Orson Hyde, 59–63; of David Nye White, 64–65; differences in, 90–92; interpreting, 113–17
Adams, George, 63
Agnosticism, 6
Allen, James B., 37
American Revolution, 13–14
Anxious bench, 120
*A posteriori* knowledge, 68

*A priori* knowledge, 68
Arminius, Jacob, 15
Assumptions and assumers, 3–4, 7, 9, 94, 115–19
Atonement, nineteenth-century views on, 15, 16–17
Awareness, in memory, 99–105

Barstow, George, 52
Bednar, David A., 86
Bible, 26–27, 89–90
Brodie, Fawn, 67, 71–74, 81, 82, 116
Bushman, Richard, 74, 108–9

Calvinism, 15
Carpenter, David, 87
Communication of Joseph Smith, 84–93
Constitution of United States, 13
Controversy, over First Vision, 1–2
Coray, Howard, 32, 44
Cowdery, Oliver, 25, 69, 78

# INDEX

Critiques of First Vision: overview of, 67–68; of Methodist minister, 68–71; of Fawn Brodie, 71–74; of Wesley Walters, 74–80; responding to, 80–83

*Cry from the Wilderness, A* (Hyde), 59–63

Dream(s), of Lucy Mack and Joseph Smith Sr., 21–22

Education, of Joseph Smith, 87
Edwards, Jonathan, 15, 121–22
Edwards, Sarah, 121–22
*Ein Ruf aus der Wüste* (Hyde), 59–63
Emotion, memory and, 96, 100–101
Enthusiasm, 71
Epistemology, 3–6, 68

Factual memories, 97, 106–8
Faith, seeking by, 113, 123–24
Fallacies of negative and irrelevant proof, 75
Family of Joseph Smith, 13–22
Finney, Charles, 119–20
First Vision: events of, 23–30, 88–92; memory in, 98–102; gaining testimony of, 111–12
Fischer, David Hackett, 75
Forgiveness, Joseph Smith seeks, 88–90, 92, 98–100
Freedom of religion, 13–14

Givens, Terryl, 122
God: love of, 121–22; nature of, 122–24

Head, versus heart, 92–93
Heart, versus head, 92–93
Hermeneutic of suspicion, 80–81
Hermeneutic of trust, 116–17
Historian(s): Joseph Smith as, 10; subjectivity of, 80–81
Historical method, 9–11, 112
Holmes, Erastus, 42
Hyde, Orson, 59–63

Insight, 108–109
*Interesting Account of Several Remarkable Visions, A[n]* (Pratt), 55–59
Interpretation of First Vision accounts, 113–17
Interpretive memories, 97–98, 105–10
Irrelevant proof, 75

Jessee, Dean C., 34–35, 44, 106n24
Joseph Smith History, *Plates 10–16*
Journal, of Joseph Smith, *Plates 7–9*

Knowledge: seeking, 3–12, 111–12; *a priori* and *a posteriori*, 68

Lane, George, 18–19, 24–25, 69, 77, 78

# INDEX

Language, as limitation in communication, 87–88
Letterbook 1, *Plates 1–5*
Long-term memory, 96–98, 101
Love, of God, 121–22

Madsen, Truman, 75
Meaning, in memories, 108–9
Memory: reliability of, 94–95; power and process of, 95–98; in First Vision accounts, 98–110
Mercy, 83
Meta-awareness, 99–105
Methodism, 14, 15, 25–26, 69–70, 77–79
Methodist minister, 29–30, 68–71, 107–8
Mourner's bench, 120
Mulholland, James, 32, 44

Negative proof, 75
Neibaur, Alexander, *Plate 18*, 65–66
Noise, 85

Oaks, Dallin H., 5

Persecution, 103, 107–8, 111–12
Personal revelation, 5
Pratt, Orson, 55–59
Priesthood keys, 34, 102–3
Process, revelation as, 86–87

Rationalism, 5–6
Record-keeping, 36, 102

Religion, freedom of, 13–14
Religious revivals: increase in number of, 14–15; impact of, on Smith family, 19; impact of, on Joseph Smith, 23–26; Wesley Walters and, 74–79
Revelation: as confirmation, 5; continuing, 29–30, 68; First Vision as, 86–87
Revivals, religious. *See* Religious revivals
Richards, Levi, *Plate 17*, 63–64
Rigdon, Sidney, 34, 44, 101–2
Robinson, George, 32, 44
*Ruf aus der Wüste, Ein* (Hyde), 59–63
Rupp, Israel Daniel, 52–53

Salvation: nineteenth-century views on, 15–17; Joseph Smith seeks truth regarding, 23–30, 88–90, 92–93, 98–100
Scientific method, 5–6
Scriptures: studying and understanding, 5; command us to seek, 7–8
Seager, Aurora, 76n21
Secondary memories, 96
Security, 120–21
Seeking and seekers: defined, 6–7; as commandment, 7–8; attitude of, 8–9; authentic, 117–18; requirements for, 121; of Sarah Edwards, 121–22

# INDEX

Smith, Asael, 13–14, 17, 21
Smith, Joseph: autobiography of, *Plates 1–5,* 33–41, 101–4, 109; 1835–1836 journal of, *Plates 7–9;* as historian, 10; history of, *Plates 10–16;* seeks truth, 23–30; on mercy, 83; understanding communication of, 84–93; trusting, 117–18
Smith, Joseph Sr., 13, 16–22
Smith, Lucy Mack, 13, 16, 17–22
Smith, William, 69, 78
Subjectivity, 80–81

Taves, Ann, 106n25
Testimony, gaining, 4–5, 111–12
Trust, 117–18
Truth, seeking, 3–5
Turner, Orsamus, 77

Understanding Joseph Smith, 84–93
Universalism, 17

Visions, of others, 118–20

Walters, Wesley, 74–80, 82
Wentworth, John, 33, 52, 101, 103–4
Wesley, John, 15, 69–70
White, David Nye, 64–65
Williams, Benajah, 77–79
Williams, Frederick G., *Plates 5–6,* 34, 34n3, 36, 37, 102, 113